mystic
lover
seeker
saint

the four paths of
spiritual awakening

mystic
lover
seeker
saint

sara wiseman

All rights reserved. No part of this book may be reproduced or transmitted in any form or by any means, electronic or mechanical, including photocopying, recording or by any information storage and retrieval system, without written permission from the authors, except for the inclusion of brief quotations in a review.

Copyright © 2019 Sara Wiseman
Sara Wiseman LLC, 4742 Liberty S #333, Salem OR 97302

Table of Contents

Preface 9
Introduction 15

PART ONE: FINDING YOUR SOUL PATH . . . 21

1 A Life Of Meaning 24
2 Our Journey Is Soul Growth 26
3 Many Paths, Same Destination 28
4 Which Path Are You On? 30
Meditation: Asking The Universe 32

PART TWO: THE FOUR SOUL PATHS 35

5 The Path Of The Mystic 37
6 The Path Of The Lover 39
7 The Path Of The Seeker 40
8 The Path Of The Saint 41

9 The Value Of All Paths 43
Exercise: Reviewing Your Paths 44
Exercise: Statement Of Belief 49
Exercise: Are You Working In Light? 55

Part Three: The Path Of The Mystic . . . 61

10 Becoming The Mystic 62
11 Sacred Study 63
Exercise: Where Do You Go? 66
12 Visioning 67
Meditation: Guiding Visions 69
13 Formal Meditation 73
Meditation: Deep Stillness 76
14 Prayer 78
Prayer: Opening The Heart 80
15 Simplicity 82
16 Bliss 84
17 Mystic Ritual 87
Ritual: Your Unique Ritual 95

Part Four: The Path Of The Lover . . . 97

18 The Three Ways Of The Lover 99
19 Bowing To The Divine 103
Exercise: Exploring Romantic Relationships 105
Exercise: Exploring Non-Romantic Relationships . . . 108
20 Sexuality and Transcendence 112
Exercise: Sexual Transcendence 114
21 Oneness Through Intimacy 117
Exercise: Opening To Others 119
22 Becoming The Lover 122

Exercise: Noticing The Lover 127

Part Five: The Path Of The Seeker . . . 129

Exercise: Awake In The World 131
23 The Hero's Quest. 134
Exercise: Your Unique Quest 136
24 The Seeker And Oneness 137
25 The Festival Effect 139
26 The Nomadic Seeker. 141
Exercise: Where Is Your Home? 142
27 Becoming The Seeker 144
Exercise: Living As Adventure 147

Part Six: The Path Of The Saint 151

28 The Saint Serves 152
29 Your Journey As Saint 154
Exercise: How Have You Served? 156
30 The Practice Of Seva. 158
Exercise: Where Are You Called? 160
31 Becoming The Saint 162
Exercise: Showing Up 163
32 Detaching From Outcome 165
Exercise: Your Responsibility To Others 167

Part Seven: The Four Paths, Redux . . . 171

33 Where Are You Now? 173
Exercise: Integrating And Understanding 175
34 Walking Your Own Path 178
35 Going Forward 180
About the Author 183

Preface

Have you ever felt that you were practicing spirituality the "wrong" way?

That what worked for others just didn't work for you?

Maybe you tried meditation—but it didn't resonate.

Maybe you joined spiritual community—but that wasn't your style, either.

Perhaps you revisited the religion of your childhood, or began following a spiritual tradition—but what you were hoping for wasn't there, either.

Yet all the while, your deep craving for a meaningful spiritual practice kept growing.

You *knew* that you could connect deeply to the Universe—if you could only find the spiritual practice that would take you there.

What you might not know is that each of us has a *unique spiritual nature*.

That means, when you stop trying to fit into someone else's idea of spirituality and start paying attention to *what works for you*, you find that having *direct connection* to the Universe—receiving Divine guidance, having heart-opening experiences, enjoying peak experiences and experiencing the bliss of Oneness—becomes your everyday reality.

It's easy. It's effortless.

And it's incredibly meaningful.

All because you've discovered your unique spiritual style.

The Four Soul Paths

In this book, we will explore four distinct spiritual paths: Mystic, Lover, Seeker, Saint—four very different ways approaching spiritual practice.

One of them, or perhaps even a few of them, will resonate deeply with you.

These four paths are really different ways of approaching spiritual practice—in fact, you might not even feel like they're "real" spirituality at all.

Yet they are. And you'll know this, because you'll feel like you've come home.

In order to discover which of the four soul paths resonates most with you, we're going to try them all out, one week at a time. By the end of your journey, you'll know clearly which soul path brings you joy, ease, happiness.

Eliminating the spiritual practices that just don't work for you is incredibly freeing.

For example, if you find that you really don't care for meditation, but you love community service, you can become free to focus on what brings you joy! If you really don't like spiritual community, but love studying Divine texts, you can approach your spiritual practice that way!

Our goal is to find the spiritual path that resonates deeply with you, that gives you the feeling that you've finally come home.

We'll walk four paths: Mystic, Lover, Seeker, Saint. As you use this book to walk each path, one per week, you will notice that trying a different approaches opens you up. So that if by nature you might be a Mystic, walking the Lover path will open your spirituality in a new way. If by nature you are a Seeker, walking the Saint path will open you further.

And as we try new paths, we become expanded.

As we walk each path, we find what works for us.

A New Spirituality

Over 70% of Americans no longer belong to the religion they were born into, according to a recent PEW report. Instead, they're taking part in something else that isn't particularly ancient or organized or traditional.

They're creating their own spiritual practice.

They're creating a religion of their own.

They're creating a spiritual belief system based on their experiences with God/One/All/Divine/Universe/Source—or any of the many other names we give to the Infinite.

It's a revolution of religion.

It's a shift in spirituality.

It's the evolution of humankind.

We are no longer following the paths of the past, because these ways no longer align with our beliefs, understandings and experiences.

Instead, we're creating our own practices.

We're walking our own paths.

And these practices and paths are as unique as we are.

✹ Certainly, spiritual community is evolving. Instead of the church of their childhood, many folks are flocking to gatherings, retreats, workshops, classes. They're reading books, listening to podcasts and connecting in online forums around the world. There's a blossoming of non-traditional spirituality.

We're all seeking the Divine. We always have been.

But what is new is that as we evolve as souls, we're understanding that there are ways of experiencing God/One/All/Source outside of religion, doctrine or dogma, and these new ways are no longer predicated on the idea that we need a leader, an interpreter, or organization to provide this direct connection for us.

Our spirituality has become personal, intimate, activated.

We understand that we can engage with God ourselves—no middleman required.

Your Unique Soul Path

There is no one-fits-all when it comes to soul work.

Just as we all have different personalities, each of us comes into this world with a unique way of communicating with the Divine.

When we are able to walk our own soul path—the path that really suits us, really resonates with us at the soul level—we can go even deeper in our connection with the Divine.

Spiritual Direction.

It just makes sense, doesn't it? Instead of trying to follow what everyone else is doing, we can instead honor our own soul's needs.

Just as some people enjoy reading while others like math, or some enjoy music while others like gardening, we all have particular ways of being in the world that are easiest, most enjoyable and meaningful to us.

Why does this matter?

When you are working in your unique spiritual style—walking your own soul path—communicating with the Universe becomes simple. There is no stress to it, no "should" or panic if you forget. You won't forget, because your spiritual path matches your soul style!

You drop out of that whole shame-based anxiety of leaving spiritual practice to the end of your to-do list, because it's hard to do, or it's confusing.

When you are walking your own spiritual path, and creating a spiritual practice that matches your own unique style, spirituality becomes the easiest, most enjoyable, most meaningful part of your life!

You engage in your spiritual practice, because you love what happens when you do. You engage in your spiritual practice, not out of doubt, or fear, or because you should. But because you find that when you are immersed in the Divine, you open the doors to love for self, love for other, love for every single thing in your life.

Every time you immerse yourself in that well of Light, you become more healed, more whole, more conscious, more awakened—and this is a beautiful way to live.

Introduction

THIS BOOK WILL help you identify your unique soul style, so that you can create a spiritual practice that works for you.

It will teach you a way of creating a spiritual practice that fills you completely—that's in alignment with who you are, and fits your most natural way of being.

No matter what religion you come from or what your belief system includes, once you discover your natural soul path, you will find it easy to have direct connection with God/One/Divine/All/Source/Universe—whatever name you use—in a way that is meaningful to you.

When you begin to explore your spirituality in a way that is easy, effortless and natural for you—that fits your personality, suits your temperament, aligns with your interests and makes sense to you as a soul in this world—you will experience a great sense of relief and joy!

No more: square peg, round hole.
No more doing what everyone else does.
No more thinking "there has to be more."
No more suffering instead of celebrating.
Instead, you'll be walking your soul path, your way.

Many Paths, One Destination

There's a saying—all roads lead to God.

When you begin to understand that you are a unique soul, here to express your individuality while at the same time experiencing your Oneness, it just makes sense that you are here to walk your own unique path to God/One/All/Universe/Source, in a personal, meaningful way.

In this book, you'll discover your unique soul path—a specific way of relating to the Universe that complements your natural personality and temperament.

You'll do this by exploring four different soul paths—Mystic, Lover, Seeker and Saint—and in practicing them all, one after another, you will discover which you prefer.

When you understand your best and most natural way of communicating with the Divine—when you start to walk the soul path that is uniquely yours—it becomes pure joy sustain a meaningful spiritual practice.

Who Is This Book For?

This book is for anyone who wants to create a personal spiritual practice based on connecting with the Divine in all the ways this can happen.

God is everywhere.

And there are many ways to experience this.

When you discover your unique soul path, you will learn how to connect with the Universe in the way that is the most natural and meaningful to you.

This book is inclusive—it can be used and adapted by people of all belief systems, cultures and practices. The only tenet in this book is the direct connection—the concept that it is our natural state to communicate directly with God/One/All/Source/Universe, in all the ways this is possible:

- *We can pray.*
- *We can meditate.*
- *We can use intuition.*
- *We can notice synchronicity.*
- *We can go on retreat.*
- *We can gather together.*
- *We can study sacred text.*
- *We can connect with nature.*
- *We can connect with animals.*
- *We can take care of each other.*
- *We can be intimate with each other.*
- *We can dance.*
- *We can sing.*
- *We can enjoy music.*
- *We can travel to holy places.*
- *We can journey to sacred sites.*

- *We can create ritual.*
- *We can find God in the small things.*
- *We can notice miracles in every day.*
- *We can witness each other.*
- *We can serve each other.*
- *We can live as soul.*

All of these are ways we can create direct connection—private, personal communication with the Divine.

If you belong to a religious tradition, this book will help you understand which parts of your tradition are most meaningful to you—what you want to focus on, what you want to deepen and explore further, and perhaps what you want to let go.

If you are not a part of a formal tradition, and aren't really sure what your beliefs are, this book will help you explore the ideas of the Divine in a new way.

If you're one of the many spiritual pioneers actively creating a direct connection with the Divine already, this book will help you understand what practices will give you the most joy and expansion.

When you learn to walk your unique soul path, you begin to communicate with the Divine more easily, more naturally and more frequently—and this of course changes how you experience your life.

How To Use This Book

In this book, you'll learn about the four soul paths, and how determine which soul path will help you create and sustain a spiritual practice that brings you meaning and joy.

The book contains Exercises to help you along the way: guided meditations, questions for your journal, and hands-on activities to try in the real world—all designed to help you explore your connection with the Divine.

Finding a spiritual style that fits you is one of the greatest joys of our lives.

As you work through this book, you'll learn how to discover the soul path that resonates with who you really are.

And from that point forward?

Your possibilities are as unlimited as the Universe.

Part One

Finding Your Soul Path

AT A CERTAIN point in our lives, the big questions kick in:

- *Why am I here?*
- *What I am here for?*
- *What is my calling?*
- *What is my purpose?*
- *How can I create a life of meaning?*

And for most of us, these questions don't come around just once.

These questions are part of a continual soul inquiry—a constant soul review of where you've been, where you're going, and where you're headed in this passage of time we call life.

If you are a conscious person, if you are aware of yourself as a changing, growing, multidimensional being, you come to these questions many times —and each time, you arrive at an understanding that is based on where you are at the moment, and what you've experienced so far.

For some of you, this question first gets answered by getting focused—you rocket forward with a sense of knowing, "yes, this is what I'm going to do!" or "yes, this is who I'm going to be!" and never look back.

For others, you answer this question by trying everything that life has to offer—you explore, meander, sample. You aren't ready to commit to one thing, until you've tried many things—and maybe you never want to limit yourself at all.

Still others of you haven't had the luxury of decision or exploration, because life got in the way—you've had to work to support yourself or others, or you were busy taking care of people, or various other life events kept showing up that had to be dealt with. You had to discover meaning in the moments between moments, catch as catch can. It's only now, when there's finally a moment of breathing room that you can even start to consider this question: what am I here for?

However, no matter what your experience of life has been until now, here's what's important to know:

Your life is not one thing.

Some of you will have one core, focused area of life's work that you do in this lifetime, such as you might invent something that changes lives, you might write an important book, or serve in an important office.

But most of you will have lifetimes that are a patchwork of many things: raising a family, building a business, being active in community, pursuing your own private interests.

No one thing matters more.

It's all important.

In fact, the most important life work you do might not have anything to do with "doing" at all. Your life's work is simply *being*, and understanding that this also has value.

Your purpose is your presence.

In this way, offering your presence in the world may be the biggest, best, most gracious and important work you can provide—by simply showing up, as a fully authentic, fully actualized human being.

What you achieve is what the world rewards. But your life is not defined only by success!

Your focus is important!

Your experiences are important!

Your presence is important!

It all matters!

Remember: there are as many ways to live and be—as many ways to discover and walk your unique life path—as there are souls!

Which brings us to another very important understanding:

Your life is how you live.

When we are intentional about our way of being—about what we put our attention to what is important to us, what we choose to experience, the quality of our presence in the world—a life of meaning seems to unfold effortlessly.

1

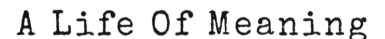

A Life Of Meaning

A WHILE BACK, I received this email:

> "How do I find out what I was created for, or what I am supposed to do while I am here on earth? I want and desire crystal-clear direction. I want to feel joy, excitement, and fulfillment! Is want to get up every day knowing that what I do matters and that someone is better for it. How can I do this?"—Anna

Anna's letter expresses the very true sense of frustration that people often have when they are ready to step fully their lives with passion and intention—and yet they aren't sure where to start. There are so many options, so many directions!

If we choose one path, will we miss out on the option for a different path?

If we don't do anything, will we get stuck?

What if we choose the wrong path?

Is there a wrong path?

These questions are important, and we can also approach them from a place of trust, instead of a place of panic or fear.

Remember: the Universe has things well in hand!

The path you seek is already there for you—all you need to do is take the first step.

2

Our Journey Is Soul Growth

WHEN WE'RE FIRST starting out on our quest of spiritual awareness, we become aware that life is a *journey of soul growth.*

No one experience will bring us to soul growth—it will take many experiences over not just one, but many lifetimes.

It can be frustrating to hear that!

It's not the hoped for response in this linear world of intention-action or goal-success. When I work with students and clients, life's purpose is one of the most common questions. "What I'm supposed to DO?" clients would ask. Or "Tell me what YOU see I should be doing."

In truth, it's pretty easy to see someone's life's purpose when we look intuitively—visions show up, and it's fairly simply to have an immediate knowing of a person's gifts, and what they're here to contribute to the world.

Yet it's not my—or anyone's—guidance to give.
No one else can reveal to you your path or purpose.
It is up to each soul to find the way.

Each person must find his own calling. Each person must step into his destiny.

This seeking itself is one of the most important parts of the journey—it's where we take responsibility for ourselves and our lives. It's where we leave all of what we're told by society, culture and family behind, and embark on a journey of self-discovery and meaning. It's where we decide to really live as authentic, conscious beings.

We leave the old ideas and identities behind.

We embark on a journey for our own truth.

We let go of the trapping and Misbeliefs of the everyday life.

We open the door to discovering who we really are, what we're made of, and why we're really here.

Not everyone will take this step toward spiritual discovery in their lifetime. In fact, most of the mainstream world will *never even desire* to do this kind of inner work, this soul inquiry.

Yet it's our only reason for being here—to embark upon the hero's quest for our true Divine self. To begin a pilgrimage to the soul.

3

Many Paths, Same Destination

IF YOU ARE daring enough to embark on this journey, there are four paths to choose from—four ways of being—that will lead you to spiritual awakening, a clear knowing of purpose, greater compassion, and an abiding sense of peace—the unshakeable understanding that all is well.

You will be living life fully, and you will have no regrets. This is what happens when you step onto each of the four spiritual paths, and begin a new way of living from soul first.

As you recall, the four spiritual paths are:

- *Mystic*
- *Lover*

- *Seeker*
- *Saint*

I haven't defined them yet, on purpose.

Don't worry—I'll define them soon. But for now, what you need to know is that each of us will walk *all four paths* in our life. Some people will *focus on one path* for most of their life, but will still have detours onto the other paths. Others will *cycle through* all four paths, one after another, many times. Others will move through the paths as a progression, staying on each path for many years.

There is no end to the variation of how we'll move through a lifetime.

4

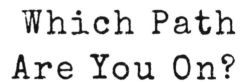

Which Path Are You On?

Do you know which of the four paths you're walking right now?

- *Are you a Mystic?*
- *Are you a Lover?*
- *Are you a Seeker?*
- *Are you a Saint?*

Even though we haven't defined what these paths are yet—even though your mind doesn't have a clear definition—your soul already has the answer.

When you connect with the Universe, rather than your mind/ego/personality, the guidance you receive can be very different than anything your mind creates—when we work from soul, the answers are always emotional, energetic and clear—you feel the truth in your heart.

In this way, answering a question from soul perspective is very simple.

You can do this by allowing yourself to meditate on your question—even if you're not sure what you're asking—and the Universe, which is all knowing and all understanding, will fill in the gaps, and will bring you understanding at the soul level—it will provide you with information that your mind/ego/personality doesn't know.

In this way, you can look into the four paths—Mystic, Lover, Seeker, Saint—right now—*without knowing anything about them.* And you can easily discover what the Universe would like you to know.

Let's try it now.

Meditation

Asking The Universe

1. Close your eyes, and take a deep breath in through the nose and out through the mouth. Breathe this way until you feel relaxed. In three breaths you will become relaxed. In ten breaths, you will be in a light trance state and ready to begin this work.

2. In your relaxed state, allow the four paths to float through your mind, one at a time: Mystic. Lover. Seeker. Saint. You can say the words aloud if you like. As you focus on each path, notice what you experience.

3. Some of you might see words, some of you might see beings, some of you might see symbols or visions, some of you might simply see colors or energy, some of you might have feelings. Don't worry too much about what's supposed to happen—

just notice what happens. In other words, just pay attention to what you start to sense, or perceive, or feel. Don't worry that you don't know the definition of these paths yet. Just allow whatever visions, thoughts, or feelings that arrive into your mind, to arrive. Don't try to think "no thoughts." Don't block anything. Just allow it all to flow.

4. Now, ask the Universe to show you, tell your, or help you feel which of these paths you are currently walking. You don't need to know anything about the paths—the Universe knows, and the Universe will inform you.

5. To do this, simply allow the four paths to float into your mind's eye, one at a time. In a very short time, you will start to settle on one path, and that path will fill your mind. Remember, you don't need to do anything—the Universe will do the sorting for you.

6. After a while, you'll notice that you won't be able to concentrate on any of the other paths—only that one path will be what you are experiencing. Mystic. Lover. Seeker. Saint. Very soon, you will find yourself settling on one.

7. This is the path you are walking right now, or are meant to begin walking right now.

8. The answer the Universe gives you may be very different than what you thought you'd receive. Allow yourself to accept this new information with a state of surprise and wonder! Or, the answer the Universe gives you may be exactly what you already sensed. In that case, allow yourself to accept this information as a clear confirmation.

9. When you're ready, gently bring yourself back to this earth reality. An easy way to do this is to count backwards from 10 to 1 aloud.

10. In your journal, write answer the Universe gave you to the path you are currently on: Mystic, Lover, Seeker, Saint. Also note what images, messages, knowings, feelings or other information arrived to you. Write about what feelings come up, as you consider this path.

11. If you've been doing soul work for a while and are familiar with this style of meditating for guidance, you probably have a clear idea of what path you're on from this meditation.

12. If you're new to this work or aren't exactly sure what you received in meditation—no problem. We'll delve further into the definitions of the four paths, so you can understand which path you're on.

Part Two

The Four Soul Paths

Now that you have your first answer from the Universe, you have a sense or knowing of what path you are walking now:

- *Mystic*
- *Lover*
- *Seeker*
- *Saint*

This path that you discovered in meditation may feel right to you, or this path may be confusing, or you still might not be sure.

Wherever you are, it's okay. It takes a while to learn how to let go of mind/ego/personality as our ruling force. So, let's take a look at what the four spiritual paths are from a more left-brain way of looking at things, so that our mind/ego/personality can catch up to our soul.

One thing to know as we begin: all of you will travel *each of the four paths* in this lifetime.

Some of you will be on one particular path for many years or decades, and walk other paths for a shorter time. A few of you will be on one path so long and in such a committed way, it may feel like that's the only path you're walking—yet this actually isn't so. At some point in your life, you'll walk them all. Others of you will walk one path for a while, and then switch to another, then to another, in a kind of cycling of experiencing many kinds of soul growth.

All of these journeys and ways of journeying are valid and good. No one method is better than the other, and no one path is better than the other. Again: all paths are valid and good. It is the destiny of each soul to experience all of these paths in every lifetime.

So, don't worry if you don't think you've walked them all yet.

The Universe will make sure you do.

5

The Path Of The Mystic

THE MYSTIC CREATES Divine connection between self and the Divine via direct connection.

The Mystic path is a solitary, introspective journey that is based on connecting directly with the Divine, one on one. The Mystic path may span many years of a lifetime, or it may be the focus during a shorter period of time. It can happen at any time in life, or you may return to this path several times. For example, you may require a period of time in which you take a break from the outer world, and go into hermitage or seclusion. Your path may involve study of spiritual traditions or esoteric knowledge—a field of study that is examined and then alchemized into a new belief system or way of knowing. However, not all Mystics will study in a formal or academic way; study may also take place through silence, prayer, meditation, retreat and being. The path of the Mystic always involves deep contemplation, quiet and reflection that create soul communion with Source. It is about connecting one on one with God.

6

The Path Of The Lover

THE LOVER CREATES Divine connection between self and other via intimacy.

The Lover is about intimacy, physicality, nurturing and caretaking. This might be sexual, as with a lover, but it can also be the non-sexual intimate connection of parent and infant, parent and child, best friends who are companions and helpmeets for each other and so forth. This may be a lifetime journey, especially for women or people who live their lives in the domestic realm of family; or it may be a journey that is for a defined period of time, such as with a lover who is a primary soul mate, or the raising of a child who is a primary soul mate, or in serving to be companion to a friend or relative in later years.

The Lover finds God in intimacy with others.

7

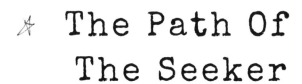

☆ The Path Of The Seeker

THE SEEKER CREATES Divine connection between self and the world via exploration.

The Seeker discovers the Divine in travel, exploration and adventure in the world. The Seeker may travel many lands, or may adventure close to home, but the result is always connection with others in the world. The Seeker creates connection via experiencing new things, looking at the world in a new way, connecting with different cultures, connecting with the past both on a historical and energetic plane, connection with the planet and the energy of different places in the world. This path may be a life path, or a period of time. The Seeker learns Oneness in exploring that which is different from self.

The Seeker finds God through being in the world.

8

The Path Of The Saint

THE SAINT CREATES Divine connection between self and other via service.

The Saint serves all he or she meets, but not out of slavery or victim role; the Saint has moved well past those fear-based or poverty-conscious roles. The Saint may walk the path of selfless service, such as volunteer work, working for no pay or service that is compensated. Or, the Saint may serve in a more fluid way, such as being of service to anyone who crosses their path. Again, the Saint understands that selflessness is not the same as enabling or co-dependency. The Saint simply shows up in compassion and non-judgment, and serves as Divine Self, in whatever way the moment requires. The Saint also understands that Seva (service) is not about fixing things or directing outcome—the Divine controls all outcome.

The Saint finds God through service.

9

The Value Of All Paths

REMEMBER, NO ONE path is better or more challenging or more elevated than the other. All paths are equal—they each bring us to the Divine. Some paths may occupy many years of your life, or you may gravitate to one path, and not explore the others very fully.

There is no particular order to the paths, with the one exception that the Saint role can't be fully inhabited until all of the other roles/paths have been journeyed at least once.

Exercise

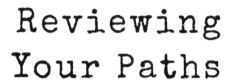

Reviewing Your Paths

You know that you'll walk all four paths in this lifetime—everyone does. So let's see what your journey has been up until now. Using your journal, review the passages of your life and the path you were on. To do this, answer these questions:

1. At first glance, which of the four paths do you think you've experienced so far? List all of them that come to mind: Mystic, Lover, Seeker, Saint.

2. Now, write down when in your life you experienced these paths. The way I like to do this, is to create a timeline of your life, with Birth on the far left hand side, and Death on the far right.

3. Next, label your timeline with key life passages, such as Infant, Child, Teen, Young Adult, Adult, Midlife, Older Adult, Elder. Now, look at those markers and remember what events were happening in your life. And from there—knowing your general life stage, and the events that you were experiencing—consider the spiritual path you were on: Mystic, Lover, Seeker, Saint.

4. For example, a common life path for an American baby boomer might be:

- *Child, loved nature and imaginative play: Mystic*
- *Teen, activities and exploring the neighborhood: Seeker*
- *Young Adult, first romantic partner: Lover*
- *Adult, raised a family: Lover*
- *Midlife, traveled the world: Seeker*
- *Older Adult, began spiritual quest: Mystic*
- *Elder, became involved in charity or mentoring: Saint*

Using this example as a framework, what paths have you walked during the core passages of your lifetime: Infant, Child, Teen, Young Adult, Adult, Midlife, Older Adult, Elder? Make a list of your ages and stages, and the paths you were on.

1. What path are you on now?
2. What path do you long to experience, but haven't yet?
3. What path do you sense will be your next?

The Path Of The Mystic

The Mystic's task is to discover the Divine through *private connection between self and God.*

This path includes:

- *Stillness*
- *Solitude*
- *Study*
- *Prayer*
- *Meditation*
- *Pilgrimage*
- *Retreat*
- *Ritual*

The Mystic path is a personal journey. It does not involve other people, other teachers or spiritual community. It is the relationship between self and God, through quieting the mind and opening the heart, in a personal and solitary way.

This path is for those who are on an inner journey that uses:

- *Communing practices such as prayer, meditation, journaling*
- *Intentional practices such as intention, ceremony, ritual*
- *Awareness practices such as energy, vibration, nature*
- *Being practices such as stillness and minimalism*

The Mystic withdraws from worldly concerns and delves deeply in the interior. The path of the Mystic is to learn to understand one's self as Divine soul, in private connection with the etheric realm, etheric beings, energies and the Divine.

The Mystic journeys in the etheric realm.

The Mystic is solitary, and the Mystic spends a great deal of time alone, in contemplation, or in practices such as writing, praying, being. The Mystic journey is interior—it is the exploration of the inner self and God.

The Mystic is deeply involved with study; not just books and learning from others, but in crafting his or her own understanding of how the Universe works and of what it means to be a spiritual being having a human experience.

The Mystic's goal or destination is to come to understanding what he or she believes, and to live from that understanding. In other words, the Mystic seeks to create a belief system or credo that is his or hers alone, and to live from that understanding.

This understanding or manifesto might change or develop over time; but this continual process of retreat and inner discovery is always part of the Mystic's way.

For the Mystic, it is not enough to follow what others have determined before. Religions, philosophies, traditions and academia are all of interest—certainly, they are a valuable history of what others have discovered, and they reveal how we have evolved in our understanding of spirituality.

The Mystic honors these traditions, and studies them for inspiration.

The Mystic, however, must personally step into the Mystery on his or her own.

In other words, you must discover your own spiritual truth—as you understand it from your own personal experience of the Divine—outside of traditions and history.

Your journey in the Mystery informs you.

Your truth is created from your personal, direct communion with the Divine.

The Mystic path takes into consideration all that you have studied and learned, but its true direction arrives from what you experience with God—both in personal contemplation, and in the synchronicities of a guided Universe.

[Handwritten note:] She dream of walking with a herd of people. They all get in a big tour bus called Amal-Happy. Mon w/ Kahl haired eyes shut the gate. I can't go. Bart looking then standing w/ 2 ms old church at the packing lot of people, couples. There is a light rain w/ orange she we dancing some with white singing caps. The big church up. I hear the hymn — in the garden all about walking + talking with the beloved, with jesus w/ the Divine leader.

Exercise

Statement Of Belief

1. What do you believe? Take some time and create a *Statement of Belief* that is yours. It may draw upon various traditions and teachings, but it should be original to you.

2. Some ways to start this Statement of Belief might be to begin with the statement. "I believe..." and write down everything that arrives to you.

3. What do you believe for sure—without any doubt?

4. Did someone else create this belief, or did you discover it?

5. In your own spiritual practice of prayer, mediation, stillness, nature, what does God/One/All tell you about what you believe for sure?

This Exercise could take a lifetime, but do it in one sitting anyway. It will give you an idea of where you are now.

This belief statement should be more than "We are One" or "Love is All" or other vague statements. These are true, but I'd like you to get more detailed.

If you're still stuck, use a template from another faith to get started. For example, Catholics use the Nicene Creed as a way of stating belief; Unity Church has something similar. You might follow them as a template. However, the belief system should be yours alone, original and unique.

It is also okay to say "I don't know" as part of a belief system. The Mystic explores and discerns. See what happens as you do this.

Here are some questions to help you put together your Statement of Belief:

- *Why are we here?*
- *What is our purpose?*
- *How does the Universe work?*
- *What is God?*
- *What happens when we die?*
- *What is the meaning of our lives?*
- *What is important?*
- *What doesn't matter?*

After you have written your Statement of Belief, do some journaling on the following:

1. Did you have a solid idea of your beliefs, or was it more slippery and hazy?
2. How different are your beliefs now, than those of childhood?
3. How different are your beliefs now, than last year?
4. Do you think most people share your beliefs? Does it matter to you?
5. What is the community or organization or religion that is closest to your belief system? If there is more than one, list them.

Here are some belief statements created by some folks who've done this Exercise. Your own beliefs may be completely different. These are provided to help you understand what you might include in your own belief statement.

> "I believe the divine is a loving energy that exists throughout the universe. I believe this loving energy is within all of us. I believe in the right and in the ability of all people to access the divine in their own way. I believe all aspects of earth are part of one network and that actions by one, or by many, affects others, often in ways we cannot immediately comprehend. I believe we have the power to affect many things with our loving intentions. I believe that we are spiritual beings in a physical body, here to learn lessons and experience life as a human. I believe we have been here many times and that when we die,

we return to the spirit realm for reflection, healing and more learning."

"I believe there is one being/source of love, light and energy. And I believe this love, light/energy is a part of all everyone and everything around us.

There are beings such as guides and angels who help us on our path and there are more beings that I do not yet know or understand. I believe we can heal ourselves physically and emotionally by ourselves and with the help of divine beings. I believe love is the most important energy in the universe, love is always the goal. God/Creator/Source loves us more than we can imagine.

I believe our thoughts impact ourselves and others physically and emotionally. Everything has energy and we can impact the energy of those around us and be impacted by the people and things we surround ourselves with. I believe nature heals and grounds us. The more we are immersed in it the more we tap into our intuition, the more it heals, and the more clearly we can think and connect with the divine. I believe we can all tune into our divine guidance when we all slow down enough to connect.

I believe we came here to learn lessons for our soul and when we die we leave our physical bodies and move back into the spiritual realm. We can choose to come back again and some of us do, many, many times."

"I believe we are spiritual beings exploring human existence, learning love in the density of the beautiful blue planet called Earth. We live through multiple lifetimes absorbing a multitude of experiences throughout Duality, to see if we can discover our source, our truest form of love, in this physical human form.

We are from other planets, galaxies, stars, and connect in the sacred library of Earth, losing parts of our awareness as we descend into the density of this reality in order to joyfully find our awareness again while fully being present in the body.

Every cell of every living thing on Earth vibrates with the source energy from which we all emerge, from the molecules in the human body to the smallest speck of dust, all vibrating, all dancing our way toward awareness and connection."

Darkness vs. Light

Whenever we discuss the Mystic path, we must look at darkness vs. Light.

This may seem unnecessary or even scary at first glance, but when you begin to delve deeply into the Mystery, you will discover that there is much to be learned. There is much to be celebrated, and much to leave alone. If the time does come that you may be faced with something dark, I would like you to be prepared.

If you flirt with darkness, even with an "experienced" guide or in a "safe" way, it may seduce you. This happens very quickly and may result in quite a battle to be free.

There are practices that are widely accepted in modern spirituality that dabble in dark. These are to be avoided. If you are involved with practices that deal with the occult, even something as innocuous as using a Ouija board, calling in random energies, séances, connecting to random Departed (as opposed to communicating with beloved Departed such as your grandparents), soul retrieval, extractions or exorcisms without proper training, using substances to create spiritual experiences, casting spells, creating enchantments, or in general anything that feels dark, chaotic, unpleasant, controlling or that leads you to a place of emotional unwellness or mental schism—please don't get involved in these activities.

If it feels dark, creepy, weird or unsafe, it is.

If what you are exploring is not wholly, 100% benevolent and Light, please don't explore these practices! It's a very big Universe out there, and there are many forces that we do not understand.

Even nature is not always pure Light. Each tree, rock, crystal, stone, twig, breeze, weather pattern holds its own energy Universe, and this may be dark, neutral or Light. Be aware of the vibration and essence of everything you come in contact with.

If you're not sure if something is Light, ask yourself if it is love.

The Mystic works with the guides, the saints, angels, Jesus, Mary, Buddha, Kwan Yin, all the entities and deities who have worked to bring Light into the world for eons.

The Mystic works in Light, from Light, and with Light alone. You can't get to the Light when you work in the dark. Working in Light is the only path that will bring you to more Light.

Exercise

Are You Working In Light?

EXPLORE THESE QUESTIONS in your journal.

1. Take a moment and consider if there are any practices, objects, icons, connections, beliefs or other that you are connected to, attracted to or dealing with, that are less than pure Light. Make a list of whatever comes up, and then discern what is pure Light, what is not Light, and what you are not sure about.

2. Look at anything on your list that is not Light. Are you ready to let go of this? Why or why not?

3. Take a look at anything on your list that you're not sure about. Holding each practice in meditation, ask it if it is Light. If you are not sure of the response, as it if it is love. If your question is not answered immediately and clearly "yes," you will know that this practice is not Light.

4. Look again at anything on your list that is not Light or love. Rid or release yourself and your surroundings of anything that is not holding the full Light vibration of love.

5. If you are having trouble doing this, there is a trigger or something that needs to be looked at. Look at this now, with the help of your Guides.

6. Does it make you feel queasy to look at this question of dark vs. Light? What comes up for you?

7. Write about a practice or system you'd thought was Light, but turned out to not be Light at all. What happened? How did you know?

8. In the next few days, be aware of practices and systems that may seem to be "good" or "okay" or that might be accepted normal in the modern world, that are not Light.

Here are some ways other people think about darkness vs. Light:

> "I worked in a healing center with a shaman for a period of time and it was a pretty difficult experience. There was definitely a light and dark to him. Many of us could see the dark but his patients could not. I didn't ever feel afraid of him but saw him more as a fraud than any-

thing. He was a good healer but other behaviors just overshadowed so much of what he did. The experience did create some mistrust for me in 'gurus' and self-proclaimed teachers but the lesson was to stop looking for teachers on my spiritual path and start trusting that it needed to be my own journey."

"When practicing Reiki on people I have seen and felt some things that felt pretty bad. At first, I was freaked out and would call my more experienced healer friends to get their impressions. Now, that I'm more used to these kinds of sightings, I send them light and do not feel nearly as nervous. I am very careful to go into each Reiki session, meditation, or work with the departed with intentions of light and the Reiki mantra 'for the highest good of all involved' very present in my mind."

"I sometimes get caught up in this skewed notion of wanting to believe that there is no evil or darkness and that all perceived 'bad behavior or occurrences' are a result of playing roles and catalysts for growth. I know there is certainly dark and that it has to exist because there is light. Duality (I'm guessing) is a main learning medium for our current 3D world. So, I get a little squeamish when I think about dark vs. light - that there really may be an existential battle for balance or one over taking the other."

"I had an experience where someone came into my home to help me 'clear the energy.' It was then I learned about energies in objects. She had me get rid of many items that I had collected, thinking they were sweet, or spiritual or whatever. She took away things from altar items to dream catchers to a piece of art I had on my wall. I was amazed how positive I felt after. I still collect little things but I meditate on them first."

"I am aware of Light and dark, especially in my travels. I make sure I either do a simple little loving ritual when I enter a new environment where I'll be staying - or just say 'any energies which are not mine, are not of love and light, must remove themselves now' or 'I release all that which is not mine.' I make a habit of claiming the space when I arrive and then cleaning it as I leave."

"Darkness has existed since the beginning of time. It is up to each individual not to follow it. I come from a family of healers and mediums, some of which practiced in dark space, through dark rituals and restrictive modalities. Very early on I listened to my heart, that voice deep inside me and decided this was not for me. I chose to respect it but not participate."

Walking The Paths

For the next four weeks, you will walk the path of Mystic, Lover, Seeker, Saint: one path each week.

The first week, you'll become the Mystic.

Next week, the Lover.

The following week, the Seeker.

The final week, the Saint.

Some of the paths may feel very easy and effortless to you; they will mirror how you are already being and behaving in your life.

Some of the paths will feel challenging, odd, expanding and even uncomfortable to you.

You'll walk each path for one week, one after the other, to discover what is like to try a new spiritual path, to get off the trodden, customary, comfortable path we've been on for a while—or even our whole life—and try something different.

The only thing that doesn't change as we walk each of the four paths, is our focus—our focus is always spiritual expansion. So, no matter if we are walking the path of Mystic, Lover, Seeker or Saint, we are always on a path with the Divine, we are always walking with Light—just in four different ways.

When we explore new paths, we notice new things.

This increases our understanding.

Part Three

The Path Of The Mystic

For this week, you will become the Mystic by adopting the habits and practices of the Mystic.

These you will build into your daily life, for one week.

Again, it might not be your usual practices, or how you usually live or like to live. That's okay. We're trying something different, changing some things up, seeing what happens when we push our edge.

Remember the Mystic is about the *personal, internal, private, direct connection* with the Divine. This is a path of slowing down, turning inward, study, journaling, contemplation, meditation and prayer.

10

Becoming The Mystic

SOME IDEAS OR suggestions for becoming the Mystic this week are:
- *Sacred study*
- *Visioning*
- *Formal meditation*
- *Prayer*
- *Simplicity*
- *Bliss*

11

Sacred Study

PART OF BEING the Mystic is study of sacred text.

Go to the library or bookstore and seek out spiritual books to study. Let yourself wander and be guided to the books that you are meant to study.

You can also do this online; simply let the Universe guide you to what you are meant to notice.

However, if you can, it is fascinating to see what happens if you simple go to a used bookstore, and start wandering the stacks, and see what you are led to. Or a library, or a new bookstore. In all cases, we want to have direct connection with the Universe, and allow the Universe to guide us. There is something about roaming the stacks and tables of a bookshop or library that allows the Universe to serendipitously let you find the right book—to allow it to catch your eye.

It is especially nice at a library, because then you don't have to make a commitment to buy anything. You can just notice what you are led to.

Allow yourself to be drawn to what you are drawn to.

In doing this practice of simply exploring and being open to possibility—of looking for what you don't know you're looking for—many people have reported synchronistic events such as books leaping out from the shelves into their arms, or books seeming to call from across the room.

I myself have experienced this many times!

Allow the Universe to attract you to what you need. If you are not sure what you are being attracted to, explore ancient or sacred text: *the Bhagavad Gita, The Tibetan Book of the Dead, Tao Te Ching, A Course in Miracles* are examples of sacred text that many people have found useful. Some of you might also like authors such as Andrew Harvey, Matthew Fox, Angeles Arrien, David Whyte, Kahlil Gibran, Rumi, Hafiz to name just a few, who all appeal to the Mystic sensibility.

Or you might be drawn to completely different authors.

The Universe will make it clear.

If you're at the library where borrowing is free, or a used bookstore where prices are low, you can load up a big stack of many diverse books. Be extravagant! Allow yourself to gather this richness of ideas and understandings.

Then, head home, and for the next week as your journey the Mystic path, spend at least an hour a day reading.

You may find reading difficult, at this time in your life.

It seems to have become a lost art for many.

There was a time when people read for a period of time day—it was a practice and a contemplation, or at the very least an entertainment, and people were used to sitting for an hour or more in concentrated attention.

Nowadays, reading complex text, such as ancient or academic work, or longer works, can feel very strange to a brain that had become accustomed to modern writing that is designed for shorter attention spans.

Even reading a real book, as opposed to using a device, can seem taxing.

So… challenge yourself!

Read, study, and immerse yourself this week.

When you find yourself getting distracted and bored because you are actually reading a complex book, take a breath, understand that you are doing this as an experiment to see what happens, and continue reading.

Notice how the act of reading itself—sitting down privately, taking time to study, taking time to understand complex ideas—actually changes you.

As you read, it will be very useful if you take notes on what's interesting. Not in any formal way—simply jot down in your journal what ideas pop out for you, or what seems important.

Go back and read passages that don't make sense, and see if you can cipher their meaning. Allow yourself to become engrossed in this stack of books that you and the Divine have chosen for your Mystic journey this week, and notice what starts to happen.

Exercise

Where Do You Go?

EXPLORE THESE QUESTIONS in your journal:

1. Where do you go when you are reading? By "go," I mean where in your mind or your awareness—where does that you that is your mind go when you are in the flow of these words and ideas?

2. What themes seem to be showing up?

3. What new ideas are you discovering?

4. How do these books inspire you or make you curious?

5. Do you like how reading makes you feel?

12

Visioning

For this week, following the Mystic path also requires that you "enter in" to Divine space to meditate and to pray, and also to become a seer for your own life—to practice *visioning*.

Some of you have traditional meditation practices, some of you have modern practices, some of you have never meditated, and some of you don't like meditating. Some of you pray by rote, some of you pray your own way, some of you don't pray.

Wherever you are, it's great to try new things!

The Mystic is all about exploring direct connection with the Divine in meditation and prayer—and in this specific practice of visioning—and thus, we will focus on this aspect.

For this week, you'll be meditating in a very specific way and for a very limited time: 10 to 20 minutes a day.

For those of you who don't have a meditation practice, this will be challenging and might even seem like too much—it may be a challenge to do this. For those of you who have a particular meditation practice, this may feel odd or uncomfortable—why do things differently? Why such a short meditation?

This is because using this particular meditation style while you walk the path of the Mystic, will help open you up in a new way. Whenever we try new spiritual practices, more of us is opened.

We try new things in order to have new revelations. We break out of habitual patterns, so that new ideas may come to light.

If you have a particular meditation practice already, or if you always meditate at the same time, or with the same group of people, you are highly encouraged to try this new practice for this week. If you feel ungrounded without your customary practice, do that too. It is never a bad thing to meditate more.

Meditation

Guiding Visions

THIS MEDITATION IS a method of gathering information from the Universe. It is inspired by a technique we use in spiritual intuition, that I call Guiding Visions.

The sole purpose of this type of meditation is to receive a Guiding Vision from the Universe in answer to a particular question.

In this way, you are asking for direct and specific guidance as you walk your path.

You are asking clear questions, and the answers will arrive to you as visions in your mind's eye, that are either symbolic or real, or potentially as movies in your mind.

These visions may take you to other time: past, future, present, or past lives and future lives, or other dimensions that are unfamiliar to you.

These visions may take you to other places: different countries, different spaces, even different planets.

Usually when you ask for Guiding Visions in this way, the objects you see will be familiar to you; sometimes however, this won't be so. You'll be provided with an understanding of what the vision is about, even if it outside of your current reality.

Some of you may also receive messages that accompany these visions; these may show up as words, or sounds, or songs, or telepathy. This may happen, or it may not. For this meditation, we are focusing on receiving visions in the mind's eye.

A Guiding Vision is usually unexpected, and instantaneous. After you have practiced this style of meditation for a while, you will discover that you often receive the Guiding Vision even before you have asked the Universe a question, or even before you have closed your eyes for meditation. Understanding how quickly this information arrives will help you "catch" it as it flies past in your mind's eye.

Let's try it now.

6. Write down three questions in your journal. These should be deep questions about your life—things you are wondering about, or trying to figure out. For example, you might ask about a relationship, or about your life's work, or the path you are on, or what your next step is.

7. Take a moment to meditate on each of the three questions, one at a time. Close your eyes, take a deep breath in through the nose and out through the mouth, doing this cycle of breathing until you feel relaxed. It might take you three breath cycles, or ten. Breathe this way until you feel you are

in a slightly woozy, relaxed, gentle trance. When you are in this altered state, bring the first question into your mind. You might say it aloud, or say it in your mind, or just think your question.

8. You will notice an image or a symbol forming in your mind's eye. You might have a sense you are "thinking" it or "imagining" it. Remember: this happens very quickly—you may have received this feeling image or "thought" while you were still doing the breathwork. If you find yourself sensing nothing or if your third eye is viewing grey or black, you may have missed the image already. Ask the Universe to pull it up for you again.

9. The image you've just seen will be both symbolic and emotional. For example, if you asked the question "What is my financial situation" you might see an image of an empty black pot, and have the feeling of ashes. This would point to some lack and stress about finances in the near future. On the other hand, if you saw an image of a beanstalk that kept growing and growing through the clouds, you would expect to have great financial abundance.

10. Take each question (from the three you choose earlier,) one at a time. Go into meditation and ask the question. Notice the Guiding Vision that pops into your head seemingly out of nowhere, either before you ask the question, right when you ask it, or immediately after you ask it. It's very fast!

11. Write down what you receive, and spend a little time journaling about what this vision might mean. What does it symbolize? What does it remind you of? How does it feel?

12. Sometimes, your Guiding Vision will take you straight into a memory about something else. This is fine. That is also part of the information you are receiving that answers your question. What does this memory bring up for you? How does it relate to your question? How does it answer your question?

13. Go on to your next question, and repeat the process.

14. At the end of three questions, come out of meditation by counting yourself back from 10 to 1. A little bit of this work goes a long way.

15. During your exploration on the path of the Mystic, plan on doing this meditation every day. Ask deep questions that really matter to you. Notice the patterns that start to emerge. Notice how your soul knows the answer, even if your mind/ego/personality isn't aware of this yet.

13

Formal Meditation

You can also partake of a formal meditation practice this week. It doesn't matter what style you choose—if you don't have a formal practice already in place, choose one that appeals to you. Whatever practice you choose, the important thing this week is to commit to the practice.

And, because you are walking the Mystic path this week, you'll need to do your formal meditation alone. That means: no meditation group, no meditation community, no listening to audio with another person's voice. This also includes: no meditation CDs, and no meditation apps.

It's just you and the Divine, without the presence other people.

This can be very difficult for those of you who enjoy the support of other souls in your meditation practice.

It's okay to try something new.

You will definitely experience new feelings and understandings, if you shift out of your customary practice.

Again: to sink into this Divine space, all on your own, with no helper, no teacher, no support of group energy—not even the guiding voice on a recording—may seem like a challenge.

It may even seem impossible.

How will you do it? How will you know what to do? What if you do it wrong?

Recall that the Mystic path is about you making direct connection with the Divine, in retreat from the world.

This is about entering deep stillness.

This is about walking a solitary path.

This is just you and your ego/mind/personality giving way to you as your soul.

In this way, for this week, your meditation will be private, solitary and will involve only you as a particular soul in human container, and the Divine.

How long is long enough to meditate? That is up to you.

I've worked with some students who meditate two hours in the morning, two hours in the evening. I've worked with other students who go upon silent retreats that take many days, and the practice is to meditate all day.

And yet...

I've also worked with students who commit to 20 minutes in the morning before they get out of bed, and another 20 minutes in the evening, also in bed, right before they sleep.

And I've also worked students who grab meditation catch-as-catch-can, 10 minutes in the car while waiting to pick up their kids from school, 10 minutes while riding on the bus to work, or 10 minutes at lunch in an empty conference room at work.

Where doesn't matter.
How long doesn't matter.
It doesn't matter how you breathe.
It doesn't matter how you sit.
The practice you choose is personal. The more important thing is that you set intention for what you would like to do, and then over the week you walk the path of the Mystic, and you fulfill that promise to yourself.

Again, the practice itself doesn't matter, although you may find you prefer one practice over another.

The commitment, and following through on that to the best of your ability today, right now, is what counts.

You might do it perfectly.

You might not do it perfectly.

But you will do the best you can, in creating your intention and following through as you are able, and that will be enough.

If you aren't sure how to meditate formally, here are some guidelines.

Meditation

Deep Stillness

1. Find a quiet, private space.

2. Sit comfortably on the floor or on a chair.

3. Close your eyes and begin breathing in through the nose, out through the mouth until you feel deeply relaxed.

4. Don't think about anything in particular, or ask a question, or have any desired outcome. Just enter in to this other dimension. Call upon God, light, love, or any other holy aspect to guide your meditation.

5. Allow all thoughts, but don't hold onto them. Just let them come and go, until they still themselves. After a while, they will settle down and you will enter a deeper state.

6. Stay in this relaxed state for 10 minutes or as long as you feel like it. Let your experience be your guide as to when to stop. If you do end up going for 20, 30 minutes or even 60 or 90 minutes, it will be wonderful. If not, that's okay too.

7. If you fall asleep, trust that you needed rest, healing, realignment or all three.

8. When you feel ready, come back to this reality and go about your day. If you find yourself stuck in the other dimension, just count yourself back in from ten to one.

14

Prayer

THE PATH OF the Mystic is to be in continuous prayer throughout the day.

What does it mean to pray?

To pray a way of speaking to the Universe—to whatever you consider God/One/All/Divine. To speak with your voice and to speak with your mind, and of course to speak with your heart.

It is a pouring out of your heart to God.

Prayer is differs from meditation slightly. In meditation you head into stillness, and you bask in that vibrational quality of Light. Meditation is not asking. Meditation is a listening to God; it is a receiving.

In prayer, you *call out to the Universe*, you make your thoughts and your voice known, you may have requests, you may have supplications.

In prayer, you speak to God, you ask God to know your heart. In meditation, you listen to God, you ask to know God's heart.

Which is better, to ask in prayer or to receive in meditation? To ask or to receive?

There is no better—both are Divine. Whatever way you choose to connect, the Universe will meet you.

And so praying is an asking, a supplication, a request—and there are so many ways to pray! Some of you will want to use traditional prayers. You may want to use prayer beads, or a rosary or some other marker of your prayers.

What is good to know about prayer is that even though the words you say may seem important—what really happens is that the Universe listens to what's said in your heart.

The Universe will hear the outpouring of your heart. In fact, you don't even have to any words at all. You can be on your knees, you can have hands clasped in front of you. Or you can be driving to work, with your heart calling out to the Universe.

Makes no matter where you are.

Makes no matter what you say.

Just like meditation—there are no rules.

Just pray, and the Universe receives your heart.

Prayer

Opening The Heart

HERE IS A way to pray this week:

1. Find a private, quiet space. This could be in an empty church, or in your home, or in nature. Whatever appeals to you.

2. If you want to make light a candle or make an offering, do this now. If you're at a church that offers this, you can light a candle. Or if you're at home, you could place a flower on a special table or altar space.

3. Sit comfortably, relax and close your eyes. If you want to hold your hand in a prayer pose, that is fine. If you want to use prayer beads, that is fine.

4. Say a formal prayer you know, such as The Lord's Prayer, or a mantra that you repeat. Or say nothing. Both are fine.

5. Open your heart to the Divine, and hold nothing back. Ask for help with whatever you need help with. Give thanks for whatever you are thankful for. If you are struggling or have a burden, ask that it be lifted. If you are confused and need clarity, as to be shown the way.

6. Stay in this state of openness until you feel a sense of peace and grace fill you.

7. When you're ready, open your eyes and come back to this reality.

15

Simplicity

MYSTICS TRADITIONALLY LIVE in small, quiet, plain spaces, and they have very few possessions. A mystic may live in a tiny hut in the forest, or in a cave in the mountains. Living simply is a part of the paring down to essence of the Mystic path.

This week, in addition to reading, ritual, meditating and praying, you will also live simply. Here are some ways to create this simple, devotional life:

- *If you have the time and space, consider fasting for some of this week, or for part of each day. Fasting is an ancient practice that can bring spirituality to the body very quickly, such as visions, trance, and lucid dreaming.*
- *Go to bed early.*

- *Get up early.*
- *Dress plainly.*
- *Live a quiet, simple life without entertainments.*
- *Spend as little money as possible. Consider being celibate this week, or if that's not possible for you, approach sex as a sacred act.*
- *Give some of your possessions away.*
- *Give up screen time.*
- *Give up mainstream interests such as politics, sports, celebrities, shopping.*
- *Give up all substances: alcohol, drugs, cigarettes, everything.*
- *Go to church, by yourself. You don't need to be a member—any church with open doors will suffice. Simply enter in and be in that space and see what it feels like to be there.*
- *Go into nature, and treat this as your church. Walk, pray, be as nature surrounds you.*

Be minimalist in all things, except your devotion.

Allow yourself to become transcendent: become one with God/Divine/All. Allow yourself to become holy, holy, holier still this week: to have a course of study, prayer, meditation, minimalism and devotion that allow you to experience yourself as a true Devotee of the Divine.

16

Bliss

It is common for this weekly practice of the Mystic to create bliss states, transcendence, and altered states. This is what the Mystic experiences—personal communion and ecstasy with the Divine.

Paring down into soul essence is very powerful work.

Because of this, you will want to pace yourself. If you find it's too much, ground yourself by going back into your regular life for a bit. For example, watch a comedy, eat some food, go see some friends, play with your kids, sleep in—whatever you need to normalize again.

Take up the Mystic path again, the next day.

When you have spiritual experiences from exploring the path of the Mystic this week, allow yourself to be fully open to feeling what you feel—let yourself have emotions, even if they are uncomfortable or different for you. Some of the emotions that are common to the path of the Mystic are transcendence, dissolving into everything, deep and unshakeable peacefulness, abiding calm, and an overwhelming sense of the beauty of everything. Pay attention to how these emotions or feelings guide you or open you to a new understanding.

Here are some thoughts from people who have walked the Mystic path.

> "I want to devour and soak in as much information as I can, from so many different sources and texts and teachers. I have a pile of books that I look at longingly, but have only a spare few minutes here and there. It always leaves me longing for the ability to stop time so I could sit and read, and pray, and meditate for long periods of time."

> "St. Theresa of Avila said "I looked for God and I found myself; I looked for myself and I found God." Security, success even happiness are illusions and fleeting at best. Wholeness is really the only goal. To be authentic, you must reclaim all the parts of yourself that have been lost or discover the ones that are latent. This is wholeness. This is a process that is only possible with a spiritual connection."

> "When I allowed myself to go into stillness, I felt like a part of me that was missing came back. As it if had been

hiding, waiting until it was safe to come out again. The Mystic path helped me coax out that still, silent part of me, which I now see is the most authentic, most powerful, most real part of me. I have been missing it all these years, distracted by life. Stillness brings it back—it brings me back."

"Coming back home to prayer was a big surprise for me. As a child I was taught to pray by memorizing prayers, and when I left the church, I left all that behind. I was afraid to pray again, after so long and having changed so much from the child I used to be. When I prayed this time, the first time in decades, I prayed from my heart, instead of by rote. It felt like I was truly praying for the first time."

17

Mystic Ritual

THE MYSTIC CONNECTS to the Divine via direct connection.

One is the ways direct connection is anchored in the physical world is via ritual.

We sometimes think ritual means practicing magic, or conjuring spells. Some traditions do use these aspects of rituals, but that's not what we're doing here.

Or, we think ritual means a lengthy process of specific celebration, done a certain way. For example, taking part in communion in a church service, is an example of a particular ritual. However, the Mystic ritual doesn't follow these patterns either.

It's *a personal experience*, created and performed by you in the way that fits your unique spiritual style. It is a way of adding some physical elements into your practice, so that you what you are experiencing is more grounded in the physical world.

You can bring elements from other spiritual practices if you want, but you don't need to. It is entirely personal—it is how you want to connect with God, in a purposeful and physical way, surrounding a particular intention or celebration.

For example, on the path of the Mystic, you may be drawn to:

- *A ritual of completion*
- *A ritual of releasing*
- *A ritual of celebrating*
- *A ritual of beginning*
- *Anything else that feels important to you.*

Introducing ritual into your spiritual practice can be incredibly powerful. Again, ritual does not have to be performed in a certain way, and does not require a lot of props or steps or complexities.

Instead, ritual can be as simple as setting intention around a particular aspect of your life, and then using the practice of ritual as a marker, pause, release, manifesting, or thanks for that particular aspect.

The most important thing about ritual, for the Mystic, is the concept of being in direct connection to the Divine while doing the ritual.

For example:

- *You start to realize you've had an unhealthy relationship or unhealthy habit for a long time, and you might be ready to release it.*
- *You spend time exploring this in the Mystic manner: in meditation, prayer, stillness, reading, walking, journaling*

or other solitary spiritual work, and as you connect to Source in this way about that particular relationships or habit, you discover that it is right and you are ready to release it. Your exploration might take a few meditations, or you might work with the Divine on this habit for many years. You will know when you are ready.

- *You decide to do a ritual as an indication or marker of your conscious intention to release this habit.*

- *Your ritual might be as simple as burning some incense, or safely burning some papers or objects that represent this habit.*

- *It might be even simpler, such as moving a rock in your garden to a prominent spot, so that you might see this rock every time you come in and out of the house, and are thereby reminded of that conscious releasing. The activity is not important. The activity is just a physical manifestation of the energy and intention you are already putting into motion.*

- *Or you might simply work within a meditation that you ground physically: instead of meditating while sitting or lying down, you might go and stand in a particular spot in nature, and invite all of the nature forces, all benevolent and beloved ancestors and Departed, and all your Guides to come and be a part of your ritual. In this swirl of sacred energy, you continue your meditation of releasing.*

- *Or you might use your voice to call in the four elements during your ritual: air, earth, water, fire. You might notice these elements arrive as energy: shifting weather, changes in temperature, a sense of profound connectedness to all of nature and all benevolent energies seen and unseen.*

- *Or you might play music or sing or chant or dance.*
- *Or you might paint or draw or create art as your bridge into Divine space, and do your ritual that way.*
- *Or you might do something different entirely, as feels right to you.*
- *In creating your ritual, you "anchor" in the body and mind, what it is you are releasing. For example, if you choose to use burning incense or a small piece of paper, or even to have a small (safe) fire, this is a physical activity that you will remember for many months or even years later. The physical activity anchors the intention.*
- *If you choose to dance, you "anchor" the ritual in your mind physically with the movements and gestures you make.*
- *If you choose to paint, you "anchor" the ritual in the physical act of painting.*
- *And so on.*

In this way, ritual might be seen as a way of marrying intention and energy with physicality—you work in the etheric realm with your intention, and you work in the earth realm with your activity.

Rituals are very useful during significant times of the year, such as Winter Solstice when we move from dark in to Light, or any of the solstices, solar and lunar eclipses, different phases of the moon, and also for marking earthly celebrations, such as when there is a birthday, wedding, graduation, etc.

Ritual at these times can be private solitary, or they can be celebratory, involving community or groups of kindred friends.

Solstice Ritual

I find it meaningful to celebrate Summer and Winter Solstice with ritual—it's something that I do personally and privately. Even if I am with family and friends on those days, I will also find some time and space on own at some point, and have a solitary ritual.

My style of ritual is very simple.

For Summer Solstice, for example, my intention is to connect with the Universe and mark the day of the year in which the planets shift from days being longest, to the nights being longest—even though it is still summer, it is the beginning of a season of rest.

For Winter Solstice, my purpose is to connect with the Universe and mark the day of the year in which the planets shift from the nights being the longest, to the days being the longest—the day we begin to have more Light.

It is, of course, a symbolic marker, celebrated for eons by many pagan and Celtic cultures, and it brings a respite from the mainstream celebrations at this time of the year that may be commercial or cultural or religious. These traditions are valuable.

But for me, Winter Solstice especially is a more somber, solitary, personal event—it's a sacred moment, to pay attention to the moment in which dark gives way to Light.

So I take time for a private celebration, and in this way I give myself time and space to wrap up my year, and to acknowledge the changes I have been through. I review what I have seen change outside of me, and what has changed inside of me.

I might start the morning with meditation—chances are good that on Winter Solstice, it's going to be cold and dark, and I will awaken in that cold darkness, and take the day as a holy day, and be open to whatever is. During meditation, I'll ask the Universe to guide me to understand how I have grown during the year, what I am actively working on, and what I need to pay attention to that I am now missing.

Later I might have some time to journal on my feelings as I look back and review the year. Years ago, my focus was on what I had accomplish or experienced, but now that I am older, my focus is on how I feel and what I've learned emotionally and spiritually.

There is a huge amount of soul growth that happens over a year's time, and I see the places of progress—as well as place where I didn't make progress—with gratitude.

Again, the ritual itself is very simple.

I head outside when the sun sets, regardless of the winter weather—snow, rain, clear—with a candle in hand, and stand under the starry sky, and say my intention aloud for the Light to come.

I don't worry what I say: I let whatever comes from my heart be spoken. If I have the sense that my body needs to make a gesture, I will do that gesture. If I have the sense that I need to call in Guides, or the Departed, or any nature energies, or anything else that needs to be there with me in that moment, I will invite those Divine beings or energies in.

If I have a candle, I will light it and watch the light shine in the dark. And then for a few moments, I will become still, I will connect to God, and I will have absolute presence for everything that is within and without me.

I will stay in this space until I feel the energy change—it is a subtle feeling, but all of a sudden I will know this ritual is complete, and it's time to go inside.

As you can see, it's so very simple.

Yet this physical act of going outside, standing under the planets and stars and marking this moment with the flame of a candle, is a profound way of anchoring intention in the body, mind and heart.

And yes, it's true: the first time you create ritual on your own, it can seem very awkward—on the one hand you might feel giddy with excitement that you are trying this new and mysterious thing. On the other hand you might feel embarrassed or unsure, or feel like you won't know what to do, or you will somehow do it "wrong."

There is no wrong, when you connect with the Divine.

Ritual for the Mystic can be simple, quirky, original—it is your own private and personal way of marking a moment or a passage.

Creating Your Mystic Ritual

To review, the Mystic uses ritual in private way—it is a solitary act, done by oneself in direct connection with the Universe. It is intentional prayer or intentional meditation—not a spell or charm or incantation. There is certainly nothing occult about it. In the Mystic ritual, no drugs or substances are ever used—the point is to have whole consciousness, not altered consciousness.

The Mystic ritual is all about the Light. The Guides, the beloved Departed and other holy beings arrive into this ritual, and are with us fully and completely. If we are in nature, we also open our connection to those essences and spirits who join with us in Light.

Consider how rituals might serve to be markers on whatever you are working on now, in your own life. These markers might be earth events, such as graduations, achievements, finishing something.

Or they might be markers in which you set intention for a new part of your journey: exploring something within that you have been afraid to look at before, or clearing yourself of something that isn't working.

Ritual

Your Unique Ritual

HERE IS HOW to create your ritual.

1. Create and perform a ritual as soon as you have the time and space—the weekend can be a good time for many people. Make up your ritual, by yourself. It can be very simple or very elaborate—there are no rules. It is between you and the Universe what you create.

2. Do this ritual privately, by yourself. Don't tell anyone what you're doing, before or afterwards. The path of the Mystic is private.

3. The day of the ritual, spend some time in meditation and in journaling, to become informed what you are working on, and what you'd like help with.

4. Go into nature for your ritual, if at all possible.

5. If you are called to say or do anything, follow what you are called to do.

6. As you enter in the energetic space of your ritual, invite any Divine beings and energies to support you. Notice the quality of how you feel, as you are in the space of ritual. Be there fully—you as your soul self, in full presence—for as long as you feel you should. When your ritual is complete, you will know.

7. Afterwards, write down what you did, how you felt, and what happened. Write down your impression of what changed internally for you—how your understanding changed or how you were guided.

Part Four

The Path Of The Lover

YOU'VE WALKED THE Mystic path, and discovered how it resonated with you.

Some of you loved it—others of you, not so much!

If you are currently on the Mystic path, it's likely that you were blissfully happy walking this path last week, and wished you could stay on it forever! You adored all that meditating, praying, contemplating, studying, ritual and becoming solitary and still in your contemplation of God. It fit you, it suited you, it felt right and comfortable and meaningful to you.

However, if you aren't currently on the Mystic path, you may have found the past week to be challenging. You might have found the Mystic path was too solitary for you—you might have found it slow or constraining or quiet.

Either way—whether the Mystic path resonated with you or didn't—you learned a lot.

And now, we are ready to explore the next path: the path of the Lover.

You'll explore the path of the Lover for the next week, and see how it resonates with you. Some of you will adore it and want to bring more aspects of the Lover into your life going forward. Some of you will find it too intimate.

Again: whatever your experience, you'll learn a lot about who you are, and how you are growing as soul.

It is in exploration that we discover.

18

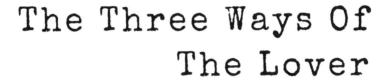

The Three Ways Of The Lover

THE LOVER'S TASK is to connect to the Divine via *intimate connection with another.*

The Lover has two modes of expression: *nurturing caretaker,* or *romantic healer.*

You may walk the path of the Lover through nurturing caretaker—through the hands-on acts of caring for another person, such as a child, partner, parent or friend.

You may also walk the path of the Lover in a romantic way—with a partner with whom you explore intimacy and sexuality.

At first glance, these might seem different—how is caretaking a child, for example, the same as a romance with a spouse?

Again, the key word is intimacy—the path of the Lover is about being close to one other person, in a way that honors them and creates Divine connection between you.

For example, you are intimate with people when you know them well, you live with them, you know them for many years or even your whole life, and you care for them, in the hands-on, every day, familiar way we take care of babies, children, our parents and our partners.

You love them.

And your love is expressed in the daily, small, hands-on things: caring, helping, supporting. If you are on the path of the Lover, you might spend your time:

- *Feeding your baby at night*
- *Helping your child get ready in the morning*
- *Picking your teen up from a friends*
- *Shopping and cooking for your family*
- *Cleaning and caring for your home*
- *Working to support your family or partner*
- *Taking care of family finances*
- *Showing up for family events*
- *Supporting your siblings*
- *Helping your father with his chores*
- *Driving your mom to the doctor*
- *Making time for your partner*
- *Talking opening with your partner*
- *Being affectionate with your partner*

- *Exploring sexuality with your partner*

You celebrate the Divine between you, by connecting to each other in these intimate ways.

If you are a nurturing caretaker, you might perform tasks such as cooking for someone, helping them get dressed, driving someone somewhere, helping them get in or out of a car, holding hands, hugging, spending time as companion, listening. The Lover in the caretaker mode is about spending one-on-one time with another person, and being a helper and nurturer. It is physical in its aspect: when you cook for someone, no matter how simple the food, the meal is infused with love. When you help someone get dressed, whether this is a very young child or a very older person, you are helping them in a way that requires patience and compassion—it is an act of love. When you hold someone's hand, no matter if this is a person you know very well, or if this is a person you are comforting, it is a gesture of comfort and connection—it is an act of love.

Thus, the Lover is all the ways you are physically close, emotionally close and a caretaker and a nurturer to others in a non-sexual way.

The nurturing Love is often something we express with family members, as we tend to live with family for many years, and are responsible for their physical care. So in this case, the role of the nurturing Lover for family might include:

- *Caring for children as mother, father, step parent or guardian*
- *Caring for elder parents*
- *Caring for other family members*

Nurturing love is of course also not limited to family—it may extend to close friends or acquaintances who we help during a difficult time. This might include:

- *Caring for a friend*
- *Taking care of an acquaintance who needs help.*
- *Taking care of anyone who needs help*

It is all about connecting deeply, one-on-one, in ways that honor the Divine in the other person and in yourself—that invite the Divine to be a part of the relationship.

The path of the Lover is for those who are on a spiritual journey of connection that intimacy as:

- *Intimacy through affection with anyone: child, relative, friend, partner*
- *Intimacy through hands-on care for another, such as a child, relative, partner, parent, someone who is ill*
- *Intimacy through transcendent sex with a spouse, beloved partner or karmic partner*

19

Bowing To The Divine

THE LOVER'S MAIN aspect is *heart connection*—it is about connecting to the Divine through heart connection with another.

The phrase "namaste" is commonly understood as "I bow to the Divine in you."

When you bow to the God in another, you bow to the God in yourself.

When you connect fully to the Divine in others through intimacy: either physical affection or intimate care in a non-sexual way, or intimate expression in a sexual way, you bow to the God in that person.

When you walk the path of the Lover—when you allow yourself to be intimate, vulnerable, connected and engaged with another person—you open the possibility of discovering the God that is in the other person, that is in you, and that also exists as an energy force between you.

Some other characteristics of the Lover include:

- *The Lover often lives with other people: a family or partner or other people*
- *The Lover may spend a great deal of time in connection.*
- *The Lover may spend a great deal of time in caring and caregiving.*
- *The Lover is a journey is of relationship.*
- *The Lover is fascinated by how we are all connected, especially the notions of relationships, karma, karmic connections, past lives, reincarnation, and ancestry.*
- *The Lover also understands the physical aspects of intimacy create and release energy—especially in sexual intimacy.*

This understanding or manifesto might change as we grow and mature; but there is something in the act of vulnerability and openness that is part of the Lover's journey.

Even if you're not on the path of the Lover now, chances are good that you have been at one or more times in your life.

Let's take a look now.

Exercise

Exploring Romantic Relationships

USING YOUR JOURNAL, explore your romantic relationships, either past or current.

1. In your journal, draw a horizontal line from left to right across the page. You are creating a timeline that shows the significant romantic relationships in your life.

2. Now, on the timeline, label your birth at the far left, and your death at the far right. You are creating a timeline that shows this lifetime.

3. Now, on the timeline, mark where you are now. Of course, none of us knows when we will die, so just pick something that feels right to you.

4. Now, label when your most significant relationships started. For example, if you met your husband in kindergarten, you would mark this in the general "kindergarten" area of the timeline, and write his name there. If you have just begun a relationship with an important lover, then make a mark that is close to now, and write that person's name down.

5. Continue this until you have all the important romantic relationships in your life marked on the timeline, with the person's name beside it. You don't need to write down all of your romantic relationships, if you've had a lot of them—just the ones that felt important to you, in whatever way you define that. For example, you may feel more connected to a brand-new relationship, than you do to an old, very long-term relationship. Or, you may feel a great surge of connection to someone you had a romantic relationship in the past. Just allow your feelings to guide you.

6. Now, one at a time, start to recall or remember each person you have marked down on your timeline, and answer these questions in your journal.

7. As you look back over the timeline of your life, which of these romantic relationships seems the most important to you? Which seems the least important?

8. Take some time, and bring up each person in your memory. What do you remember right now, about each of these relationships? Write down what comes to mind about each person.

9. Take some time, and bring up each person in your memory. What do you remember right now, about each of these relationships? Write down what comes to mind about each person.

10. What are the karmic lessons you learned in each relationship? Write down your answers for each person. Another way to look at this question is, what did you learn from each person?

11. What are the soul gifts you received from each person? Write down whatever comes to mind.

Exercise

Exploring Non-Romantic Relationships

Using your journal, explore your non-romantic relationships, past and current.

1. Create a new timeline, and use this timeline to do the same process for your non-romantic relationships.

2. Label when your most significant non-romantic relationships started.

3. Continue this until you have all the important non-romantic relationships in your life marked on the timeline, with the

person's name beside it. As a guideline, most people will have anywhere from one to ten relationships labeled. This could include family, friends, work associates.

4. Now, one at a time, start to recall or remember each person you have marked down on your timeline, and answer the following questions in your journal.

5. As you look back over the timeline of your life, which of these relationships seems the most important to you? Which seems the least important?

6. Take some time, and bring up each person in your memory. Write down what comes to mind about each person.

7. Take some time, and bring up each person in your memory. Write down what comes to mind about each person.

8. What are the karmic lessons you learned or are learning in each relationship? Write down your answers for each person.

9. What are the soul gifts you received or are receiving from each person? Write down whatever comes to mind.

10. And now, answer these questions: Do you feel you are on the path of the Lover now? What are the relationships that are significant to you now?

11. If you do not currently have a romantic partner, do you feel this will return for you? Why or why not?

12. If you do not currently live with others in domestic relationship, do you feel you will do this again?

Here is what others on the path of the Lover experienced:

> "I feel that I am on the path of the Lover right now, with the care of my children, relationship with my husband, and in being a teacher. There's a lot of caretaking going on for me right now, caretaking of others mostly. In going over the Lover lessons, I've come to terms with some painful things. So, I can't say that I've enjoyed this lesson much, but the revelations are important for my own growth. I've realized I don't do nearly enough self-care to ensure that I'm operating from as full of a cup as I can. More space needs to be created for my own health and well-being."

> "I've realized that my life right now (and probably for a long time) consists of giving, giving, giving. Of all of my energy. To other people who don't necessarily care what I expend on them energetically. I'm not sure what this means for me aside from that I need to be mindful of when people are requiring too much of me, and that it's appropriate too for me to expect an energetic return or exchange."

> "I was blessed with being in two long-term soul mate relationships. During these relationships I experienced great soul growth through the lower vibrations such as suffering and betrayal. I have grown to appreciate and

cherish those experiences because I can finally understand that the purpose of those relationships was soul growth. I learned about true intimacy, forgiveness, self-love and having the courage to walk away from toxic energy. Although I am no longer in relationships with these individuals and do not have contact with them, I am grateful for having had them in my life. Without them realizing it, they gifted me with immense wisdom through adversity."

"My non-romantic relationships with family and friends have served the purpose of soul growth. Although some of these relationships no longer exist or are currently limited, they allowed me to learn about myself in profound ways."

"I am not currently on the path of the Lover. That was my prior path and may be a future path but for now, I am cherishing the lessons I learned while in that path. The most significant relationships I currently have are with my colleagues and friends and I am learning to relax in the state of happiness/contentment. I feel that in the future I will meet another soul mate and I consider myself being marinated by the Divine for that experience."

20

Sexuality and Transcendence

HUMAN SEXUALITY IS one of the most Divine experiences available to anyone.

First, the act of creation is Divine at a level that cannot even be fathomed.

Creation is a true miracle—how a new being is called into existence via the connection of two beings. This connection calls in the new soul to be born into a human experience.

Obviously, our sexuality is not only meant for reproduction! We are designed to connect—physically and energetically—in the profound way that sexual intimacy with another allows.

As you think about sexuality and transcendence in terms of the path of the Lover, what you'll want to remember is this:

- We are each energetic beings. When we connect deeply with another, our energies or auric fields merge. Sometimes this appears or is sensed as a cloud of energy between two. The energy is palpable, sensory and may be visible to some. Sometimes it presents as golden or white light or flooding of light.

- A way to think about this might be aural blending or merging, such as the merging of the energetic or subtle bodies of each person.

- It is common in sex for people to experience past lives, astral projection, losing sense of time and space, becoming someone different.

- Sexual intimacy is a kind of a trance, and it creates a portal for going to different places in time and space.

Exercise

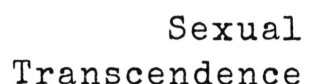

Sexual Transcendence

EXPLORE THESE QUESTIONS in your journal.

1. Have you ever had a past life or transcendent experience during an intimate encounter? What happened?

2. Where did you go or who did you become?

3. Have you every sensed a cloud of energy or aural merging during an intimate encounter? Did you see it or sense it?

4. Do you think intimacy heals?

Here is some sharing from others.

> "Intimacy, especially sex, makes me panic. And as a result of not engaging with my husband, we're growing further and further apart. I feel like it would not be possible for me to experience transcendent intimacy or sex based on my emotional damage at this point. It sounds wonderfully spiritual, but I feel that it would be outside of what I'd be able to surrender to at this point in my life, or ever."

> "I have been fortunate enough to experience transcendent sex in this life time and it was a powerful experience in which I was filled with immense heat and energy. The energy generated during the encounter was like a huge ocean wave. I sensed an aural merging that was intensified outside of the sexual encounters."

> "I have experienced a cloud of shimmering energy that seemed to hang over my partner and myself, and fill up part of the room. The energy cloud, or whatever it was, stayed over us a long time, maybe ten minutes. It felt as if the energy between us had become so elevated, that it had merged—as if our auras had merged into a third energy, and turned into golden light."

"Often when I am having sex, I go into a dream state where I don't know who I am. I don't consciously try to do this, it just happens. I seem to inhabit other bodies— people who I was in past lives—even though I am also aware I am with my partner now."

21

Oneness Through Intimacy

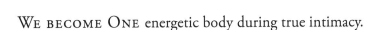

WE BECOME ONE energetic body during true intimacy.

Of course, we are One already—separation is a myth. And yet we forget this, going about our daily lives, with our various ideas and concerns.

True intimacy, either sexual or non-sexual, opens an energetic passage or portal between us, allowing us to easily merge into Oneness. This portal can take place when one or more of these aspects are present:

- *Physical touch*
- *Emotional availability*
- *High emotional states (joy, grief, etc.)*

- *Recognizing the Divine in another*
- *Connection to the Divine in another*
- *Transparency and openness*
- *Vulnerability and trust*

Again, these aspects aren't necessarily romantic or sexual. For example, you could have a moment of Oneness helping your child draw a picture, or looking at old photos with an elder parent.

Practitioners who work in energy and healing often experience Oneness with clients; it's the nature of the energy exchange.

In fact, you could have a moment of Oneness with any random person you met, if the level of emotional openness or transparency was there.

Take a look now, at your own experiences in your life. Look especially at how willing you have been to open yourself to another, physically, emotionally.

Exercise

Opening To Others

EXPLORE THESE QUESTIONS in your journal:

1. How vulnerable have you been willing to be? With who?
2. How transparent are you with others in general? With people you trust?
3. How has your ability to be open changed over time?
4. What do you think "transparency" is? How does it show up in your life?
5. How vulnerable were you in your 20s? How vulnerable are you willing to be now?
6. If we did not have bodies, how transparent do you think our souls would be to each other?

Here is some sharing from others.

> "I protect myself so much, for fear of ramifications of true transparency, being myself. The thought of being left behind because of who I am and how I feel is scary. I suspect this is behavior that I've learned through my adolescence and early adulthood. For a long time, I believed my self-worth was attached to what and whom I have in my life. I know this isn't true, of course. But still, it's a hard habit and thought pattern to break."

> "I am more willing to be vulnerable now than earlier in my life. I've realized there is nothing to lose by being as true to ourselves and our beliefs as possible, but I am definitely a work in progress in this way."

> "I was vulnerable with my past partners, family members and friends and those experiences were filled with trepidation at first but with time I eased into the highest levels of intimacy. I have been a guarded person and take the time to observe my surroundings. As I expand in soul growth, I am slowly beginning to allow myself to become unhinged, to be free with physical and emotional contact thereby becoming transparent."

"In my younger years up to my 20s, I was free and open, but after experiencing low vibration, I took a step back. I have healed from those experiences and now welcome the opportunities to experience intimacy, love in all levels."

22

Becoming The Lover

THIS WEEK, YOU'RE going to walk the path of the Lover. Remember: the Lover is about intimate connection with another. This can happen one of three ways, via:

- *Intimate emotional and physical connection and sex, such as in romantic love.*
- *Intimate, non-sexual and non-romantic connection, such as in hands-on care of another person: a baby, a child, an elderly person.*
- *Embodied, grounded connection with yourself, as a physical being.*

For this entire week, you're going to be the Lover in as many ways as you can.

The Romantic Lover

This week, you're going to explore being the romantic Lover, in one of three ways:

- *If you're not in a romantic relationship, the Lover invites you to re-open to this part of your life. This could mean going on a date, or it could mean just considering the idea of opening to that possibility.*
- *If you're in a romantic relationship now that feels flat, dull or problematic, the Lover invites you to bring more vulnerability, openness, love and passion to this relationship... and to see what happens when you do that.*
- *If you're in a romantic relationship now that is already connected and passionate, the Lover invites you to go further: to become more open and vulnerable with your partner; to show up truly naked in the relationship.*

Take a moment now, and figure out which category you're in:

- *Not in a relationship*
- *In an unhappy relationship*
- *In a happy relationship*

The Lover suggests that you open yourself more fully, and learn to create more connection to another person. Depending on your situation, you could:

- *Allow yourself to be in a sexual relationship.*

- *Learn about tantra or kundalini energy.*
- *Make room for more sex in your relationship.*
- *Become more vulnerable or communicative in sex.*

Or maybe it's not about sex—maybe you could be more emotionally open with a partner, outside of sexual intimacy. For example: What does it mean to drop all our hurts and angers and armors, and truly connect with another soul? What does it mean to stop hiding from our partner: to stop the fear, lies, avoidances, regrets, grudges, hurts that get in the way of true connection?

In other words: how much armor can you take off, how naked can you show up, how can you be truly intimate with a lover or partner?

Again, the idea is how much can you open up? Not how much connection your partner can return—this may or may not happen. But how open can you get, how naked can *you* get, how much can you show up as soul?

As in: How affectionate can you get, how truthful can you be, how emotional can you be, how much can you express your true desires, your true dreams?

This is for you to explore this week.

Note: There's no right or wrong way to do this. And of course, this work will trigger some of you, maybe most of you. It is not a simple thing to shift a lifetime of hiding and projection, and show up as the naked, true, real self in a relationship!

For some, the path of the Lover can be extremely difficult!

It can be incredibly scary to open up to romantic love again; to go through the vulnerability required to go on a date with someone.

It can also be incredibly scary to explore the Lover in a relationship that is wounded, and these efforts may not fix anything. In fact, it may help you see even more clearly that a relationship can't be fixed. That is often painful.

However, in relationships that are on solid ground, walking the path of the Lover can be incredibly freeing and expanding for both partners.

The Non-romantic Lover

The path of the Lover is also non-romantic intimacy. You will be asked to take care of other beings in a non-sexual this week.

This aspect of non-romantic intimacy is great for those of you with family nearby.

If you don't have family relationships nearby you might simply seek out some people that you can take care of in a hands-on way: a neighbor you can cook dinner for, a person you can visit at their home, someone you can invite in for tea, someone you can take on an errand, and so forth.

The idea is to spend intimate, quiet, personal connection with another.

Look for ways to share a private, small, everyday moments with another person. This will be when you are relaxed and doing normal everyday tasks: cleaning, cooking, helping.

It could be as simple as holding someone's hand. Hugging someone. Helping someone in a small way. Be hands on, present, and open.

Note: this kind of intimacy with others can be an absolute delight, and it can knock your socks off, if you are haven't been in this state for a while! Be present, and be blessed.

The Lover Of The Self

Finally, there is a third way to be on the path of the Lover. You are asked to love yourself this week! To be hedonistic and physical in your enjoyment of your body, in all the ways this can be! This shows up in all manner of self-care. You might consider:

- *Getting a massage*
- *Doing exercise you love*
- *Taking a long bath*
- *Walking barefoot outside*
- *Going to ecstatic dance*
- *Hugging everyone*
- *Painting your toenails*
- *Cutting your hair a whole different way*
- *Buying new clothes or getting rid of old ones*
- *Swimming, skinny dipping, hot tubbing*
- *Cooking, eating amazing foods*
- *Napping, sleeping, resting*
- *Whatever sounds fun to you*
- *What feels nurturing to you*

How can you be physical, intimate and connected to yourself? What brings the fully embodied 'yes' to you?

Exercise

Noticing The Lover

EXPLORE THESE QUESTIONS in your journal, and notice what comes up for you as you consider the path of the Lover.
What part of the Lover did you find most difficult?

1. What was the easiest?
2. What surprised you?
3. What changed during this journey?

Here is some sharing from others.

> "Napping, sleeping and resting have been the most surprising occurrence as I allowed myself to caretake my Self. With this particular restful sleep have come massive

amounts of dreaming and communicating with living and past beings. Before I began my dream nirvana, my spirit guides prepared me. They told me it's work you need to do."

"I held hands with my daughter. It has been almost 10 years since we held hands; the last time was when she was small. It felt like a thunderbolt. It surprised me that something so simple could be so important."

"I had a discussion with my partner about our sex life, and my desire to be more open. We ended up have a several-hours discussion, not about intimacy, but about some topics in our lives that we'd both been avoiding bringing up. It was very clearing. I felt like we reached a new level of trust with each other."

Part Five

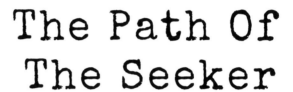

The Path Of The Seeker

THE PATH OF the Seeker is for those who are on a spiritual journey of expansion that uses travel, adventure and exploration as a way of:

- *Seeing new things*
- *Letting go of judgments of "one right way"*
- *Experiencing compassion for humanity*
- *Experiencing compassion for the planet*
- *Detaching from old routines*
- *Being fully present in all experiences*

- *Embarking on a hero's quest*
- *Understanding what is "home" and what is "away"*
- *Understanding we are always home*

The Seeker's main aspect is *outward expansion*—in understanding one's self as Divine, and in connecting full to all the Divine the world has to offer: places, people, cultures, histories.

The Seeker may spend a significant period of his or her life traveling; it may be a life choice and way of living, or something that is a passion.

The Seeker is fascinated by the many ways that souls inhabit the world.

This is the Seeker's experience on the spiritual path—to learn and grow from outward expansion in the world.

Curiosity, compassion and acceptance are a part of the Seeker's journey.

Chances are good that you've been on the Path of the Seeker at one or more times in your life. Let's take a look now.

Exercise

Awake In The World

EXPLORE THESE QUESTIONS in your journal.

1. Go back into your memory and locate one of the first trips you ever took.

2. Were you by yourself or with others?

3. Was the journey for personal, business, family, political or spiritual reasons?

4. Did you begin the journey thinking it was for one thing, but it turned out another way?

5. What do you remember about this journey? Go into your memory, and pull out one tiny slice of that experience. You will be surprised by what comes to mind.

6. Was the time frame in which you traveled (childhood, teenage years, adulthood) significant? Why?

7. If you have not traveled much, where have you traveled to?

8. How does this smaller excursion shape your life?

9. If you long to travel, where do you want to go?

10. Do you find these memories or longings arrive from past lives?

11. What attracts you about these places—describe them in detail, as if you were there now.

12. Do you find that you are able to astrally project yourself to distance places, both in present and different times? Try it now.

Here is some sharing from others.

> *"My first trip was a volleyball trip to California when I was 17. I remember being so excited to finally GO somewhere! My family was not wealthy and my mom worked nights, we never vacationed, ever. We stayed in Manhattan Beach and I soaked up every minute of it. I remember the feeling of sitting on the beach on the ocean, feeling free and like the luckiest person on earth."*

> *"I always astrally project to a place that seems like Tibet. I see mountains and open fields, lots of color in the buildings, and smiling happy people. Oddly I'm not cold!*

Another place I often travel to in my mind is Bali—that's probably because I got to go there once and loved it. There is something magical in the air that attracts me to tropical places. The depth of the greens in the rice fields, the way people dress and eat, the way they live outside all appeal to me."

"Cuba was a difficult, stunning place for me. As much as I loved the people and the music, the culture and intelligence, I had a hard time being there. Both times I went there I got sick, and the second time I got so sick it took over a year to get better. I feel lucky to have climbed out of it. I also felt really sad there. Like a deep old sadness. I could never figure that part out."

"I didn't travel until I was in my 40s. I grew up in a small town, and never really left that community. For many years my life was all about family. Nobody I knew traveled, either. When I finally took a trip, I was surprised how easy it was. I had been taught all this fear about strangers, but I didn't feel afraid. It felt like a big world out there. It felt like there were a lot of ways to live, not just how I was raised."

23

The Hero's Quest

THE SEEKER EMBARKS on *the hero's quest.*

This idea of the individual setting out, leaving home and facing challenges that he or she must overcome is the classic tale of Homer's Odyssey, and almost every popular movie out there.

The idea is that we're never the same after the trip—we grow into a new person.

And, there's something about this leaving home and returning home, that bring the Seeker's expansion full circle.

For example, Dorothy in *The Wizard of Oz.* She went on a trip, faced all kinds of challenges such as apple-throwing trees, poison poppies, flying monkeys, and the ultimate Bad Witch who she was required to defeat. All of those challenges, just so she could learn "there's no place like home."

If instead of looking at the movie's moral as "stay home and be safe," instead we look at it as "you are always home, all the time," or as Glinda the Good Witch put it... "you've had the power all along, my dear..."

The saying "You can never go home again" refers to the idea that you can return home, but you are not the same person as you were before you took the journey.

We can do the hero's quest, and in the expansion that takes place on our trip, we change, we grow, and if we are very lucky, we learn that we are always at home, in our own skins, wherever we are.

In spiritual language, the human body travels and journeys over a lifetime. But we're always at home in our souls, wherever we go.

Exercise

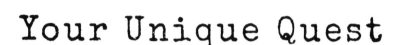

Your Unique Quest

EXPLORE THESE QUESTIONS in your journal.

1. Write of a journey that was a hero's quest for you. What did you learn? What had changed when you returned home?

2. Write of a time when you learned how to be "home" wherever you found yourself.

3. Is this true for you now?

4. In spiritual terms, what is the symbolism of the ruby slippers?

5. When was the last time you journeyed on a hero's quest? Do you feel the need to do this soon?

6. Are you in the phase of heading out (becoming the Seeker) or heading home (moving from Seeker to another path)?

24

The Seeker And Oneness

EVERY TIME WE leave "home," we leave the shelter and the routine of that place.

Perhaps we enjoy a certain kind of coffee every morning; but when we travel, this coffee is not available.

Perhaps we normally are in a certain weather system, but when we travel, the environment, flora, fauna and weather are all different.

When we journey even more exotically, we come to places where almost everything is different; the language, the terrain, the food, the way of dress, the customs, everything.

The only thing that remains the same for us is our humanity.

This ability to look across all outside aspects and to see the collective soul that exists in all humanity—this is one of the key ways the Path of the Seeker is a spiritual path.

At first, in our journeys, we may only see difference—these may be shocking, enjoyable, scary—we may have a range of responses. As we move further into our journey, we see only sameness.

- *That we as humans are all unique.*
- *That we as humans are all the same.*

Both views, held simultaneously. Which eventually morph into the spiritual understanding of soul, of Oneness, of being one of One.

25

The Festival Effect

IF YOU'VE EVER been to a festival where people wear costumes or outfits—where I live in Oregon, FairyFest might be a good example. People dress up in wings and outfits, and they spend a lot of time creating these extraordinary costumes.

When you first arrive at the festival, you're sort of stunned by it all—there's a woman wearing wings, there's a man in another outfit, and so on. It seems a different world! You can't believe all the things you're seeing. When you enter the festival gates, you can't believe what you're seeing—it's all so wild and new.

But after you've spent the afternoon there, you've grown accustomed to the new reality. A person walks by dressed like a green fairy, or a dragon, or whatever it is, and you don't even blink.

In fact, when you exit the festival, you laugh at the faces of those newcomers now entering, who can't believe what they're seeing!

The idea is that in the moment you looked with fresh eyes, you were looking from a state of full presence. You were in heightened awareness of everything: not just how things looked, but how they sounded, smelled, felt, etc.

Travel, even a small trip, helps us look at things in a new way—it's another way of crossing into awareness. It's a way of coming out of ego self, and looking with the bigger view.

26

The Nomadic Seeker

SOMETIMES, WE TRAVEL too much. This lack of rootedness is not the same as being home in our skins. When we keep on the move (and this might be with trips, but it also might be with jobs, relationships, whatever it is, always pressing to the next thing) we forget to be at "home" with our selves.

In modern world we have the ability to go from one place to the next. It's easy, it's distracting, it keeps us running and this may make us feel that we are on the right path. But even nomads are known for the way they return to certain places within the seasons. These places are touchstones, where they can gather and remember: I was this way last time I was here. I was this person, when I was last in this space.

The Seeker path is sometimes portrayed as glamorous, rich, fulfilling—but it is just another path; just one of the ways we can learn.

Exercise

Where Is Your Home?

EXPLORE THESE QUESTIONS in your journal.

1. Is there a time you have been nomadic in your life? What was your experience of always being on the move?
2. Is there a time you needed to leave "home"?
3. Is there a time you needed to return or reclaim "home"?

Here is some sharing from others.

> *"I feel that I've been nomadic for the last few years, but truthfully it feels like much longer than that. Looking for 'home' has been a big issue! I feel that I am getting close to a place, but I also recognize that the home I seek is inside*

of myself. I also must admit that at this point putting down roots, taking my possessions out of storage, staying put and beginning a more regular work schedule is a bit scary at this point."

"After living in the same house for almost twenty years, I finally gave it all up. Now, I've moved several times in the last two years. I'm living out of boxes. I don't feel connected from the community around me, which is different from the way I was so involved in the past. At the same time, this temporary living feels okay. I don't need to know where I'm going yet."

"As a kid, I moved almost every year. That meant a new school and having to make new friends. I learned how to fit in very quickly. I sometimes wish I'd had the roots that others I know seem to have had growing up. I am confident in my ability to live anywhere, but at this point in my life, I don't want to."

27

Becoming The Seeker

THIS WEEK, YOU will walk the path of the Seeker.

If you have a lot of family or work responsibilities, you will want to prepare ahead or get those taken care of as much as possible.

The Seeker is about being out and about, exploring and being in community as much as possible. This might not feel comfortable for those of you who are deeply introverted and need your home and alone time. It's just for a week. See how far you can go.

Ideally, as the Seeker, you would be traveling the world, visiting different cultures and communities, and being a global citizen... a person who is at home anywhere he/she is.

However, since most of you don't have tickets for a trip around the world in your back pocket, we'll do the Seeker path closer to home. Even in familiar settings, the Seeker can be very exciting and expanding.

Again, the idea is to be out and about: with others in community, away from all that is private and solitary. Depending on your work and family responsibilities, you might do this by:

- *Going to a community event every single night or most nights, for a week.*
- *Taking a road trip on the weekend, in which you preferably stay overnight outside of your home.*
- *Couch surf somewhere else a few nights during the week.*
- *Go to festivals or community events, such as all the summer festivals where there are crowds of people.*
- *Go to coffee houses, bars, galleries, stores—anywhere there are lots of people all the time.*
- *Try new ethnic foods, visit new places, try new experiences.*
- *Dressed for exploration, like you might if you were a world traveler carrying everything in a small backpack.*
- *Show up and connect with what you discover. Don't hide with a book or laptop. Talk to everyone you meet.*
- *Fill every moment with being in the mix with people, all kinds of different people, all the time, as much as possible during the week.*

For some of you, this will be heaven. You love getting out, getting in the mix, rubbing shoulders with Collective Soul. If that's you, go crazy with it! See how much stuff you can pack into this week!

For others of you, this will be extremely challenging. For introverts, the Seeker is a hard path; it doesn't provide the privacy and solitary time that an introvert needs.

So, if the Seeker is a difficult path for you, make it easier. Go out three nights in a week, and call it good. If you need to head back home and recharge with privacy and quiet time, do that. If you need to take someone with you on your adventures in the world, do so.

But do make the effort.

You may find, as you get used to being "out" that you can do this much more easily than you think. Keep pushing yourself out there more than usual, and see how it feels, and what you notice.

Exercise

Living As Adventure

1. All this week, explore, get out and do new things, travel if you can. You may be too busy to journal much this week, but that's okay. This week is about doing and connecting. When you do get a chance, reflect on your experiences.

2. What did you learn about your own ability to become one of One?

3. What did you learn about yourself as separate or connected to others?

4. What was hard?

5. What was easy?

6. What else did you notice?

Here is some sharing from others.

> "I took a trip to Sedona for my Seeker week. I thought it was funny that I had planned a vacation months ago and now it was occurring during the Seeker week. I went to a spa and had a facial, a vacation activity for sure, and while in a deeply relaxed state had a vision of a Native American woman holding out her hand and inviting me to join her. She was smiling like she knew me and was happy to see me. I saw myself as a boy or a man, riding like the wind on a beautiful horse. I saw an older man, a shaman I believe, and a teepee with other women and children around. I felt very comfortable there. The next day I did a jeep tour and the guide was a lovely man who recited an Apache poem to us about dealing with life's struggles. It was a beautiful moment."

> "It has been hard for me to become one of one while being part of a group I am traveling with. It is hard to carve out time to just be. Many agendas and always on the go is not a great way to connect with spirit. However, if I am always open to the possibility of connection I can get messages in places I would never expect, in the ordinary activities of my life."

"I define myself as an introvert, so I was concerned the Seeker path would be overwhelming. What I found out was that it was a lot of fun. I went to a community concert in the park, and it was great to watch all the different kinds of people. To my surprise, I felt filled up, instead of depleted."

"Being asked to be on the Seeker path for a week was the excuse I have been looking for! I did a road trip, and planned several stops each day. I felt completely in flow, free from the regular routine and responsibilities. I woke up every morning in a different place, super excited to see who I would meet and what might happen. Needless to say there were too many synchronicities and surprises to mention. It was great!"

Part Six

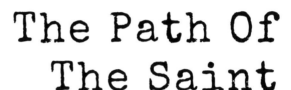

The Path Of The Saint

THE PATH OF the Saint does not mean you must be "perfect" or "holy" or "never eats chocolate" or "never drinks beer" or whatever the judgments we might have about what is saintly and what is not.

The path of the Saint isn't about inner actions. It's about *outer service*.

For example, you could be a whiskey chugging, cigar smoking, financially devious person who is acting in Seva or service to others and this is fully path of the Saint.

This can be hard to understand, because of course we want to become more integrated—ideally, we want the outer Saint to reflect the inner Saint and vice versa.

But sometimes we develop the outer aspect, and the inner has to catch up. Or again, vice versa.

28

The Saint Serves

THE PATH OF the Saint is for those who are on a spiritual journey of service which includes:

- *Service as a way of helping others with the most basic humanitarian needs: food, shelter, medical care.*
- *Service as a way of moving the self aside; of becoming selfless through service.*
- *Service as the path of helping through action.*
- *Service as way of discerning what is "self" and what is "other" and how these both are One.*

The Saint's main aspect is service or Seva—in moving one's own needs aside to serve another in action. Again, this is not only about "helping" others, or being nice to people, it's about service as a way of living a life, and service as doing.

Becoming selfless or transparent in active service is the main aspect of the Saint's journey.

29

Your Journey As Saint

Even if you're not on the path of the Saint now, you may have served in this way already.

There are times we are the Saint, and times we're not.

For example, when my children were young I was on the path of the Saint for about 12 years. During this time, I served on about five boards or community organizations, I helped at the church, did community service, etc. This was my path for a long time, and I was very busy with it.

And then one day, I moved into the path of the Mystic.

The path of the Saint was done for a while.

No, I have been on the path of the Mystic for 16 years, and I cannot yet see an ending of this path in site. It will happen, but for now it is my path.

That was my experience, but yours may be different. Some people are Saints their whole lives, such as of Mother Theresa—someone who inhabits Saint as their primary life path. They are in the world; they are all about service.

Others may be a Saint at one time, then take a break, then return later.

There are many ways to walk this path.

Let's take a look now.

Exercise

How Have You Served?

EXPLORE THESE QUESTIONS in your journal.

1. When have you been the Saint? This might be community service, charity, missionary work, helping the poor?

2. Did you do this as a child? As a teen? During what other times in your life?

3. When have you taken a break from the Saint? Look back at where you were, when you moved from Path of the Saint to another Path.

4. Do you feel awkward or have trouble with the idea of the Saint? Write about how this is for you.

5. Are you being called to walk the Path of the Saint now? Write about how this feels for you.

6. Write about a time when you walked the Path of the Saint. Share this in detail: what you did, what it felt like, what you learned.

30

The Practice Of Seva

SEVA MEANS SERVICE.

This means active service, helping with basic humanitarian needs: food, shelter, clothing, medical care. This can also mean ecological needs: disaster, toxicity, plants and animals.

There are so many ways to walk the path of the Saint. Some might be:

- *Traveling to an orphanage and helping*
- *Supporting the Red Cross*
- *Disaster relief*
- *Helping at a church or community center*

- *Gathering food and clothing for the poor*
- *Serving at a clinic*
- *Helping clear debris and pollution from the earth*
- *Planting trees*
- *Starting a foundation*

I'm sure you can think of many more.

Not everyone has the personality to do all aspects of the Saint.

For example, some people might be very comfortable gathering warm coats for a coat drive. Others might find it easy to travel to help with disaster relief. Others might want to help the ecology, or animals.

Exercise

Where Are You Called?

1. Write a list of what areas of Seva would you like to help with.

2. If now is not the time to walk in Seva, what Path is most important for you to be walking (Mystic, Lover, Seeker)?

3. Sometimes we perceive that "saint" is better than any other way. Can you see that all paths are worthy, and one is not better than the other? Write about this.

4. Who do you know in the world, that you consider a Saint, doing Seva?

5. Who do you know in your community, that you consider a Saint, doing Seva?

6. Who do you know in your family, that you consider a Saint, doing Seva?

Here is some sharing from others.

"I decided to plant trees! I have never done this, and I decided it would align with my values to support the environment. I went, there were about 10 people there and we planted a lot of trees! It was hard work but it was fun and satisfying to me personally."

"My first choice was to volunteer at an equine therapy ranch, but to do that you needed training so I did my second choice which was walking dogs at the animal shelter. It was harder work than I expected, because some of the dogs are really big and have a lot of energy from their kennel time. I am a die-hard animal lover, and I have recommitted to animal protection after this experience."

"As a stay-at-home mom with a three-year-old and a baby, I wasn't sure I could fit the Saint in, but I gave it a try. I signed up for something we could all do together, and we ended up manning a volunteer booth for a children's event for several hours. It was fun, and the kids did great. I am not sure I would do this again, as I think I'm more on the path of the non-romantic (and actually also the romantic) Lover right now, but it was a good perspective."

31

Becoming The Saint

THIS WEEK YOU will walk the path of the Saint.

You will live in Seva (service).

You can do this as a volunteer, or helping with charities, as part of your path this week. But no matter what activity you choose, your intention will be to show up to every single person that you meet or connect with this week, in service to their soul.

You show up to the person on the bus, to your boss, to your partner, to your child, to your parent, to your friend, to your enemy, to the person you wait with in line, to the person who junk calls you on the phone.

Every single connection, you show up as the Saint, in Seva.

Exercise

Showing Up

YOU'RE GOING TO show up to every person you meet as the Saint, all week long.

1. For one day, keep track of every single connection you have. Just jot it down in a notebook or takes notes in your phone. This includes people you come across in person, by phone, electronica, etc. Any time there is an energetic connection. At the end of the day, recall each person that you were in contact with, and explore these questions in your journal.

2. What happened during your one day keeping track of your connections as the Saint?

3. What surprised you?

4. What did you learn?

Here is some sharing from others.

> "For my Saint week, I decided to volunteer at a local community multicultural event. It wasn't directly helping people in need, but it was helping the community in general. What surprised me was how many different cultures reside in our town. I met a lot of different kinds of people, from all over the world. It felt good to be supporting other people, and bring awareness to their culture."

> "I tagged along with my friend who is one of the key volunteers for a group in town. Wow, was she busy! She is managing entire teams, as a volunteer. It was inspiring to see how much she gave to others, and also how much this gave to her. It sets her on fire!"

> "Volunteering is something I did when I was younger, but I guess I burned out. I haven't participated in a long time. My Saint activity was spending a Saturday helping at an organization. In truth, I didn't feel that connected to it. I couldn't put my finger on why, I guess it felt like I should be doing something else. It was good to realize that my studies as the Mystic are what I truly want to be involved with in this part of my life."

32

Detaching From Outcome

ONE OF THE tricky things that can happen when you are on the path of the Saint, is that we can fall into the trap of overhelping.

We see so clearly what others need.

We have a deep calling to be in Seva.

We feel good when we're helping.

And yet when we overhelp, we do not really help others or ourselves. We fall into the trap of creating codependency an imbalance in the relationship.

You know the saying "Give someone a fish, and they eat for a day. Teach someone to fish, and they fish for a lifetime." This is exactly the framework we want to maintain, when we are on the path of the Saint.

There are no rules to this. These are choices you have to make for yourself.

For example, if you see a hungry person, the Saint will give that person food. A hungry person needs food. If you meet a person with a mental illness, the Saint will provide them with patience and understanding. A person with a mental illness needs compassion.

But what if it's more complicated—what if someone you know needs all kind of help, and you give them help, and then they just want more help. They don't have any intention of helping themselves, they want to continue to take from you.

So there you are, peacefully being the Saint, except in this case, it's not really Seva to the other person. It's actually preventing them from being on their own soul path, and working through their own soul lessons.

Again, there are no hard rules. Sometimes we are the Saint for others, even when it does create codependency or overhelping because this is just what needs to be done at the time. We have karma with them that needs to be completed.

So, as you explore your own approach to Seva, this idea of overhelping is something you can keep in mind.

Exercise

Your Responsibility To Others

EXPLORE THESE QUESTIONS in your journal.

1. What do you think is your responsibility as a soul, to helping others?

2. When is the right time to lend a hand, and when is it the right time to let go?

3. Is this different for business, for friendship, for children, for the elderly, for the sick?

4. In the past, who did you try to help, who you couldn't help?

5. In the past, who did you try to help, who you did help?

6. Are you able to be in Seva while detaching from outcome?

Here is some sharing from others.

"I had an uncomfortable experience years ago, when I began assisting my elderly neighbor. I started by doing some small things for her, like moving items she couldn't lift. This was fine for a while, but I noticed that I would stay longer and longer on my visits, and stopping by more frequently. I realized that this neighbor needed more care than I could provide, even to the point of living in a care facility. It was a very painful process, to watch her decline. I felt I wasn't doing enough, but I also wasn't sure if my helping was the right thing to do in the big picture, as it prevented her from getting the care she needed."

"I like to volunteer. I love working with others on a team, and making a difference in people's lives. This feels energetically clean to me, to work as part of a charity organization. Other times when I have tried to work directly with people I meet, it's always backfired in some strange way."

"Growing up in the city, I was taught to be cautious of homeless people on the street. For this week of the Saint, I decided to examine that belief and see if it was true. I had cash at the ready, and when I crossed paths with a homeless person, I gave them the money. It was small amounts, $1 or $15. The reactions were different than I expected. Some people took the money and didn't say anything, but one man shouted at me. It was a humbling experience. It made me look at my own ideas of who needs help, and who I think needs help."

"It has the greatest joy for me to teach kids to read. It really opens their worlds up and gives them a sense of self-worth. I go to the school once a week and work with first graders one on one. Many of them do not have English as a first language, so the skill is especially important. I love this path of the Saint!"

Part Seven

The Four Paths, Redux

IN THE LAST four weeks, you've walked four different soul paths. You've walked:

- *The path of the Mystic*
- *The path of the Lover*
- *The path of the Seeker*
- *The path of the Saint*

Some of these paths were easy for you, some very challenging. In trying the different paths, you were able to expand your consciousness, and to see where you might need some practice expanding further.

Now, we'll integrate what you've found. This will help you understand how far you have come, and help you see all the ways you have moved internally during this journey.

33

Where Are You Now?

As you've explored the four paths, you've done a great deal of both inner work and experiences in the real world.

You've learned how to connect with the Divine in a personal way. You've learned how to connect to others more intimately. You've learned how to see yourself not as separate, but as the same as others. And you've learned the value of Seva as a spiritual practice.

You may be better educated, further along, have it more together, be more expanded than some of the people you know. Or, maybe they are further along than you. It doesn't matter where you or they are: what matters is that you are able to look at the process with compassion: for them, for you, for the experience we are all having on this earth.

Now, I'd like to you look even further into your heart, and recall what you have moved through, discovered, learned, and integrated.

We'll be doing this not with the questions that you might normally ask yourself, but with questions that are more like a soul inquiry—questions we might ask a soul to answer, at any point in a lifetime.

Exercise

Integrating And Understanding

EXPLORE QUESTIONS IN writing, twice. For the first go round, answer these questions as a "speed answer." By this, I mean write down whatever comes to mind first—your "top of mind" thought.

1. What did you once believe?
2. What do you believe now?
3. What do you believe you are as Self?
4. What is your true essence?
5. How do you believe this, while at the same time still existing in the world?

6. Do you believe in other entities, such as guides, angels, departed, others?

7. Do you believe in energetic portals?

8. Do you believe in past and future lives?

9. How do you integrate soul and body?

10. What parts of your life have you moved beyond, released?

11. What hopes or dreams have you let go?

12. What hopes or dreams still hold?

13. Is it important to accomplish a dream?

14. Is it important to simply be?

15. Is it important to be good?

16. Is it important to love yourself?

17. Do you love yourself?

18. Is there anything you need to change?

19. Is this true?

20. What is the focus of your life, right now?

21. What is your greatest passion?

22. What else?

23. What do you have left to accomplish?

24. What do you have left to experience?

25. What do you have left to understand?

Now, go back and answer each of these questions again, but this time take as long as you like, and answer them fully. Break the questions up into sections if needed, and take breaks in between. If you have resistance to a particular question, that's okay. Allow yourself to be resistant, and answer the question anyway.

34

Walking Your Own Path

WE CAN ONLY walk our own path.

- We can walk as a Mystic, Lover, Seeker or Saint.
- We can walk alongside of another.
- We can walk ahead, or behind.
- We can lend a hand to those who are struggling.
- We can grasp a hand, from those who are ahead of us, and who extend their hand to us.

But we can't walk the path for another. Not even if we really love them.

Not even if they're our spouse, partner, lover, mother, father, child, sister, brother, best friend, business partner, etc.

Not even if they really need our help.

No matter how much we care.

We can only walk our own path.

Most of you have already come to this understanding for yourself. Or, you might be working through it now.

As you have walked the path of Mystic, Lover, Seeker and Saint in these last weeks, it's become clear that you must do you own soul work.

The journey of your life as a soul is about becoming more conscious and more connected. It's about finding the Divine all aspects of your life. And it's about expanding more every single day: you get holier, you get wiser, you get kinder, you get more patient, you get more compassionate, you learn to really, truly love.

You can walk any of the paths to get there, or you can walk all of the paths.

The key is to keep walking.

35

Going Forward

I HOPE YOU have enjoyed your experience of working in the four soul paths. I am certain that you've had your eyes—and hearts—opened to new ways of being, as you tried out these four different ways of connecting to God/One/All/Divine/Universe.

Now you know which path fits you best, you can build your spiritual practice around that path, at least for now.

Remember: we all change, and what we find meaningful also changes over a lifetime. So if you enjoy being the Saint now, and that really fills you up, then do that until it doesn't fill you up any more. At the time, you'll be called to be on a new path.

Or, if you're very content as the Lover right now, do that until you feel called to explore a different path.

Each of the ages and stages of our lives will bring the desire for a new experience, and new way of opening your heart to the Universe.

Finally, if you feel you are walking two paths at once: you find you love being a Lover, but you also need time as a Seeker—then build that into your life, and if you can't figure out how to build that in, ask the Universe to help you.

Nothing brings more joy to our Guides and Angels and all the Divine beings and energy who continually support us, then watching and witness our continued commitment to our own spiritual quest—our own soul journey.

The more we connect to the Divine, regardless of which path we are currently on: Mystic, Lover, Seeker, Saint, the more we gain understanding of the love and infinite possibility of this amazing Universe, and our connection to it.

Thank you for reading

Mystic Lover Seeker Saint

Sara invites you to share your thoughts and feelings:

Continue on to learn more About Sara Wiseman

About the Author

SARA WISEMAN is a visionary spiritual teacher and award-winning author who has taught tens of thousands of students worldwide via her many books, courses and training. She is the author of:

- *Messages from the Divine: Wisdom for the Seeker's Soul*
- *Writing the Divine: How to Use Channeling for Soul Growth & Healing*
- *Your Psychic Child: How to Raise Intuitive & Spiritually Gifted Kids of All Ages*
- *The Intuitive Path: The Seeker's Guide to Spiritual Intuition*
- *Living a Life of Gratitude: Your Journey to Grace, Joy & Healing*
- *The Four Passages of the Heart: Moving from Pain into Love*

- *Intuition, Cancer & Miracles: A Passage of Hope and Healing*
- *Daily Divine: Inspirations for a Soul-Led Life, Book One*
- *Daily Divine: Inspirations for a Soul-Led Life, Book Two*

Sara is the founder of *Intuition University*, and is a top contributor to DailyOM. She writes the award-winning Daily Diving blog, hosts the *Ask Sara* and *Spiritual Psychic* podcasts, and has released four healing CDs with her band Martyrs of Sound. She lives in Oregon with her family.

Connect with Sara at

www.sarawiseman.com

Return to review link

For more information about Sara Wiseman's work in spirituality and intuition, please visit

www.sarawiseman.com

Made in the USA
Columbia, SC
11 January 2021